Emily Bernard

Black Is the Body

Emily Bernard was born and grew up in Nashville, Tennessee, and received her PhD in American Studies from Yale University. She has been the recipient of grants from the Ford Foundation and the National Endowment for the Humanities, as well as a W. E. B. Du Bois Fellowship at Harvard University. Her essays have been published in journals and anthologies, among them *The American Scholar*, *The Best American Essays*, and *Best African American Essays*. She is the Julian Lindsay Green & Gold Professor of English at the University of Vermont.

www.emilybernard.com

Emily is available for select speaking engagements. To inquire about a possible speaking appearance, please contact Penguin Random House Speakers Bureau at speakers@penguinrandomhouse.com or visit www.prhspeakers.com.

T0036188

ines our obligation to our ancestors and our children, to friends and colleagues, to those who ought to know better and those who don't, while remaining ever vigilant in the act of caring for our own self. I couldn't put it down."
—Julie Lythcott-Haims,
author of *Real American: A Memoir*

"*Black Is the Body* is one of the most beautiful, elegant memoirs I've ever read. It's about race; it's about womanhood; it's about friendship; it's about a life of the mind and also a life of the body. But more than anything, it's about love. Running through this finely written, carefully considered narrative is a golden thread of understanding that what will save us in the end is true love—mature, giving, mutual, constant, and sanity-restoring love. I can't praise Emily Bernard enough for what she has created in these pages."
—Elizabeth Gilbert,
author of *Eat Pray Love*

"The essays in this collection are about Bernard's experiences of race: her life as a black woman in Vermont, her family's history in Alabama and Nashville, her job as a professor who teaches African American literature, and her adoption of twin girls from Ethiopia. It begins with the story of a stabbing in New Haven and uses that as a springboard to write about what it means to live in a black body."
—Book Riot

"Devour this book. . . . Engaging and just plain enjoyable. It offers thoughts you'll want to turn over in your own head. This is a book to tell about." —*The Miami Times*

Black Is the Body

STORIES FROM MY GRANDMOTHER'S TIME,
MY MOTHER'S TIME, AND MINE

Emily Bernard

VINTAGE BOOKS
A Division of Penguin Random House LLC
New York

FIRST VINTAGE BOOKS EDITION, DECEMBER 2019

Grateful acknowledgment is made to Amistad Research Center for permission to reprint "Incident" by Countee Cullen. From the Countee Cullen Papers Collection at Amistad Research Center, New Orleans, Louisiana.

Several of these essays appeared in slightly different versions in the following journals: "Teaching the N-Word" in *The American Scholar* (Autumn 2005); "Scar Tissue" in *The American Scholar* (Autumn 2011); "Mother on Earth" in *Green Mountains Review,* vol. 27, no. 2 (2014); "Black Is the Body" in *Creative Nonfiction* (Spring 2015); and "Interstates" in *The American Scholar* (Spring 2017). "Teaching the N-Word" was reprinted in *The Best American Essays 2006.* "Mother on Earth," "Black Is the Body," and "Interstates" were Notable Essays in *The Best American Essays 2015, 2016,* and *2018,* respectively.

The Library of Congress has cataloged the Knopf edition as follows:
Names: Bernard, Emily, 1967– author.
Title: Black is the body : stories from my grandmother's time, my mother's time, and mine / Emily Bernard.
Description: First edition. | New York : Alfred A. Knopf, 2019.
Identifiers: LCCN 2018022594 (print) | LCCN 2018034693 (ebook)
Subjects: LCSH: Bernard, Emily, 1967– | African American women—Biography. | African Americans—Social conditions—21st century. | United States— Race relations. | LCGFT: Autobiographies.
Classification: LCC E185.97.B337 (ebook) | LCC E185.97.B337 A3 2019 (print) | DDC 305.48/896073—dc23
LC record available at https://lccn.loc.gov/2018022594

Vintage Books Trade Paperback ISBN: 978-1-101-97241-0
eBook ISBN: 978-0-451-49303-3

Book design by Soonyoung Kwon

www.vintagebooks.com

Printed in the United States of America

For my daughters, Giulia and Isabella,
who lead me through the world by the hand, saying,
"Come on."

Interviewer: Then black is a state of mind too?
James Baldwin: No, black is a condition.

—*Esquire*, July 1968

The body is not a thing, it is a situation:
it is our grasp on the world and
our sketch of our project.

—SIMONE DE BEAUVOIR

Contents

Beginnings

This book was conceived in a hospital. It was 2001, and I was recovering from surgery on my lower bowel, which had been damaged in a stabbing. A friend, a writer, came to visit me in the hospital and suggested not only that there was a story to be told about the violence I had survived, but also that my body itself was trying to tell me something, which was that it was time to face down the fear that had kept me from telling the story of the stabbing, as well as other stories I needed to tell.

I began to write essays. The first one I published was "Teaching the N-Word." Over the next few years, more essays followed, along with several attempts to write about the stabbing. I couldn't tell that story yet because I didn't know what it meant. It took seven more years for me to understand that the experience of being at the wrong end of a hunting knife was only the situation, not the story itself; it was the stage, not the drama. In *The Situation and the Story: The Art of Personal Narrative,* Vivian Gornick writes: "The situation is the context or circumstance, sometimes the plot; the story is the emotional experience that preoccupies the writer: the insight, the wisdom, the thing one has come to say."

The setting of "Scar Tissue," which is the essay I eventually wrote about being stabbed, is my gut; the blood let flow by the knife is the trail I followed until I discovered the story, which is the mystery of storytelling itself, and how hard it is to tell the whole truth. Each essay in this book is anchored in this mystery, in blood. They are also rooted in contradictions, primary among them being that the stabbing unleashed the storyteller in me. In more than one way, that bizarre act of violence set me free.

But, of course, the stabbing has been a source of misery as well as opportunity. For instance, I suffered from recurrent, excruciating stomach pain for many years before another trip to the hospital revealed that I had developed adhesions in my bowel. The surgeon was able to untangle my intestines and scar tissue, but he warned me that the adhesions would return. There was nothing I could do to prevent or predict them. "You're just unlucky," he said sympathetically. The pain, he assured me, would be random and severe. It did return, thundered, again, throughout my body, and sent me back to the hospital, where a third surgeon ceded to the inherent mystery of the malady and confessed that medicine was more art than science. The gift of his honesty was, to me, as valuable as any solution to the problem would have been.

Once I accepted the randomness of the situation in my bowel, life took on a new urgency, and so did the desire to understand it. I turned to art over science, story over solution. I found a voice. The book imagined in 2001 began to take shape in a need to know, to explore, to understand, before it was too late. Insofar as the personal essay is, at heart, an attempt to grasp the mysteries of life, the form made sense to me on a visceral level. The need to understand, in fact, was what engendered the stabbing in the first place: I met the knife head on. Something in me just needed to know.

Each essay in this book was born in a struggle to find a language that would capture the totality of my experience, as a woman, a black American, a teacher, writer, mother, wife, and daughter. I wanted to discover a new way of telling; I wanted to tell the truth about life as I have lived it. That desire evolved into this collection, which includes a story about adoption that is as pragmatic as it is romantic; a portrait of interracial marriage that is absent of hand-wringing; and a journey into the word "nigger" that includes as much humor as grief. These stories grew into an entire book meant to contribute something to the American racial drama besides the enduring narrative of black innocence and white guilt. That particular narrative is not false, of course, which accounts for its endurance, but there are other true stories to tell, stories steeped in defiance of popular assumptions about race, whose contours are shaped by unease with conventional discussions about race relations. These other true stories I needed to explore, but I was mainly driven by a need to engage in what Zora Neale Hurston calls "the oldest human longing—self-revelation." The only way I knew how to do this was by letting the blood flow, and following the trail of my own ambivalence.

I was not stabbed because I was black, but I have always viewed the violence I survived as a metaphor for the violent encounter that has generally characterized American race relations. The man who stabbed me was white. But more meaningful to me than his skin was the look in his eyes, which were vacant of emotion. There was no connection between us, no common sphere, yet we were suddenly and irreparably bound by a knife, an attachment that cost us both: him, his freedom; me, my wholeness. Revisiting that wound has been a way of putting myself back together. The equation of writing and regeneration is fundamental in black American experience. So, if race was not an essential factor in what brought me into contact with a hunting knife, I have certainly treated the wound with the salve that I inherited from people whose experiences of blackness shaped their lives as fully and poetically as it has shaped mine. I am most interested in blackness at its borders, where it meets whiteness, in fear and hope, in anguish and love, just as I am most drawn to the line between self and other, in family, friendship, romance, and other intimate relationships.

Blackness is an art, not a science. It is a paradox: intangible and visceral; a situation and a story. It is the thread that connects these essays, but its significance as an experience emerges sometimes randomly and unpredictably in life as I have lived it. It is inconsistent, continuously in flux, and yet also a constant condition that I carry in and on my body. It is a condition that encompasses beauty, misery, wonder, and opportunity. In its inherent contradictions, utter mysteries, and bottomlessness as a reservoir of narratives, race is the story of my life, and therefore black is the body of this book.

Black Is the Body

Scar Tissue

I have been telling this story for years, but telling is a different animal from writing. In the telling, I have shaped a version of it, one that fits neatly in my hand, something to pull out of my pocket at will, to display, and to tuck away when I'm ready, like a shell or a stone or a molded piece of clay. The story I have honed over the years is as neat as my scar; it is smooth, and tender, and conceals more than it reveals.

Here is how the newspaper tells the story:

STABBING SPREE SENDS 7 TO HOSPITALS

Seven people were wounded, two with life-threatening injuries, when a man pulled a knife at an Audubon Street coffeehouse late Sunday and began stabbing people.

The attack, occurring about 10 p.m., caused pandemonium and a virtual blood bath at Koffee? at 104 Audubon St.

There was no apparent provocation, police said.

The two victims most seriously hurt were covered with blood, and it was difficult to tell how many times they were stabbed, police said.

"There was a lot of blood," said Detective Sgt. Robert Lawlor. "There were some very serious injuries."

Bloody handprints were visible on a window, where one of the victims apparently climbed out. Numerous trails of blood led from the coffeehouse, which is in the city's arts district, near the Creative Arts Workshop and Neighborhood Music School.

"We have no idea what provoked him," Lawlor said. There were about 10 people in the coffeehouse at the time, he said.

—*New Haven Register,* Monday, August 8, 1994

The first time I read this article I laughed when I got to "blood bath." Blood bath? It sounded like something from a trailer for a slasher movie. But it wasn't a movie, and there *was* a lot of blood, evidently, although I don't remember that part. I remember it differently:

On the night of August 7, 1994, I walked into a coffee shop called Koffee? on Audubon Street in New Haven. I was a graduate student in the American Studies program at Yale, and I was there to work. I had James Weldon Johnson with me, specifically his 1912 novel *The Autobiography of an Ex-Coloured Man,* about which I was writing a paper. I was having a hard time concentrating that night so I went to Koffee?, which was not far from where I lived, and was one of the many spaces in New Haven where students went to read and write and talk. It was a typical coffee shop in a typical college town.

I was frustrated with my work, so frustrated with my inability to concentrate that I was giving the evening only one last chance. It was late, nearly nine o'clock. Maybe too late, maybe just call it a night. I debated with myself, walking slowly the three yards from my car to the door of Koffee?. I was probably talking to myself, as I do all the time, muttering about all I had to do. A man on a bicycle and I approached the door at the same time. Beside him stood an average-size, average-looking brown dog on a leash. The man was listing on his bike, rocking side to side, as if he himself had not made the commitment to go inside the shop (*maybe, maybe not*). Our eyes met. He looked like Gallagher, the 1970s comedian—the same long hair and bald pate, the same thick moustache. Or at least that's what I remember. To this day, when I think of Daniel Silva, I think of Gallagher, whom I rarely—if ever—thought about before that night.

I don't remember who went in first, but I remember making the decision not to let the oddness of this stranger bother me. Because he was odd. It was the way he was listing on his bicycle; it was the unsettling way he looked at me. His look was familiar, or too aware—not the passing glance of a stranger. Even now, I have a hard time describing it. He was odd; it was instinct. I *knew* something was wrong with him. Or maybe this is just the cliché of hindsight speaking. After all, we're talking about a university town, and a coffee shop full of nerds off in their own odd little worlds, people who routinely talk to themselves out loud, as I had been doing that night.

Here I have lingered longer than I lingered in that moment, which passed as quickly as a proverbial blink of an eye. I looked at the man, made a quick unconscious association with Gallagher, went in to get my coffee, and planted myself at a table. I put my keys on the table. I pulled out my book and notepad. I took off my glasses and my watch. No distractions, just me and the page, as naked as I allow myself to get in public.

At some point, I looked up and noticed that the strange man had settled into a chair not far from me. I was aware of him as he watched a table full of young girls next to me, presumably undergraduates. They were talking about a sexual encounter one of them had had recently. The girls were loud, sexy, and full of swagger. I had been feeling annoyed by them and their devil-may-care bluster, but now I looked up and saw that the man was staring at them, obviously and, apparently, salaciously. I felt intimidated by his frank stare, but I looked at the girls and they didn't seem to care, which made me proud of them, and emboldened for myself. Go ahead, talk about sex, I thought. Don't let this freak scare you. Eventually, the girls left.

When they did, the man turned his attention to a young woman I imagined to be a medical student or a law student, judging by the size of her very official-looking textbooks. She tried to engage him in conversation. She said something like "Hi." I didn't hear his response, but I do know that not long after this exchange the woman gathered up her books and left.

What happened next? Here's what I told Detective C. Willougby at 1:30 a.m. on August 8, 1994 (for whatever reason, Detective Willougby recorded this in all-caps):

THIS DETECTIVE THEN SPOKE WITH
_____ WHO STATED THAT SHE WAS
SITTING INSIDE THE RESTAURANT

WHEN A WHITE MALE CAME IN WHO
HAD A DOG. SHE THEN STATED THAT
HE WALKED THE DOG OUTSIDE AND HE
THEN RETURNED. HE THEN PULLED OUT
A KNIFE AND STARTED STABBING PEOPLE
IN THE RESTAURANT. SHE STATED THAT
HE STAB [*sic*] HER ONCE IN THE STOMACH
AND SHE THEN FLED THE RESTAURANT.
SHE STATED THAT SHE HAD NEVER SEEN
THE WHITE MALE SUBJECT BEFORE AND
SHE DOES NOT KNOW HIM.

I remember stillness, the hum of low voices and the lights, bright yet soothing, like the talk surrounding me. People talking and laughing quietly. Students, professors, writers; I was the only black person present, but these were people just like me, who looked like me. So many moments like these over the years in coffee shops in so many cities; all forgettable, ordinary, and uneventful. But these particular moments on this particular evening stay with me more palpably than any other moments from that long night. The stillness, the quiet, the hum of low pleasant talk. The sensation of being inside of those moments—it is the only *real* memory I retain from that night. Yet, just beyond the borders of that quiet, pleasant memory, I can still hear the rhythmic, continuous sound of a dog barking outside, like a warning.

Suddenly, chaos. Pandemonium. Bedlam. Topsy-turvy. Madhouse. A holy mess. All hell broke loose. The room turned upside down, on its back, inside out, went crazy, flipped out. Other words, other clichés. Fear erupted like a seismic shift in the Earth's surface, and then charged and pierced and saturated the room like smoke. Fear—a good friend to me that night—chased me toward the back door. But even in the midst of this utter confusion, I paused and listened for gunshots—this was America, after all. I paused, not only to listen for the gunshots but to brace myself—literally tense my shoulders, grit my teeth, and search inside somewhere for the pain, for the tearing impact of a bullet. When I completed that brief inventory and discovered no bullet, I was overcome by a feeling of relief. Hope, luck. A chance. And a door right behind me—and I *ran*.

And then I was outside in the back of the coffeehouse. There were no lights; it was as dark as the bottom of a pocket. Others rushed by me—I don't remember if they were speaking, shouting, screaming, or crying. What I remember is silence, which seemed inexplicable to me even then. I would find out later that what occasioned that queer silence was adrenaline pounding in my ears and deafening me.

I don't know how long I watched others rush past me before I walked back toward the coffee shop. I don't remember how long I stood there, trying to understand, before everything in me *rejected* what I saw, and I charged back into the shop to retrieve my watch, my keys and glasses, so that I could drive home. Why did I do this? It doesn't make any sense. But however I try to explain it—my stubborn West Indian heritage, a Freudian state of denial—the same thing happened next.

I found myself face-to-face with the odd man, and he had a knife in his hand. At this point the knife would have had a substantial amount of blood on it. I don't remember the blood. I do remember asking him not to kill me. I meant it, of course, but at the same time it just seemed like the thing to say. I felt I was playing a role; I felt that the die was cast. I had turned and met my fate. But I was watching as much as I was experiencing. My witnessing was involuntary. In *The Autobiography of an Ex-Coloured Man*, the anonymous narrator recalls being "fixed to the spot" while he watches a white mob lynch a black man. Like the narrator, I was fixed to the spot.

Why? I did not move because I did not want to excite this man. I did not move because I had to see what was going to happen next. I did not move because I was afraid. I did not move because I was free from fear, as many report feeling in the moments before death. I did not move because I knew he would hurt me if I did. I did not move because I knew he would not kill me. I did not move because I didn't believe he had the knife I saw in front of me. I did not move because I did not know what to do. Maybe all of the above, maybe none, maybe some combination—I will never know for sure.

I saw the knife before it entered me. What was the sensation upon impact? I don't remember. But I do remember that when he pulled it out of my gut, I fell to the ground. What did it feel like? Strange. Weird. Unusual. Lying on the ground, I beseeched God for help. When I neither felt nor heard a thundering reply, I started to laugh. I knew that I needed a hospital, not God. But I call this a "God moment" anyway, because when I laughed, my wound gaped open, and I looked down and saw and then felt the thick, warm blood rush over my fingers. It is time to get to a hospital, God was saying. I got up, and ran again.

I was more afraid of being in the dark without my eyeglasses than I was of running into the man with the knife again. I have been wearing glasses since I was eight years old. The last time I had gone without my glasses in public, I was not allowed to walk down a street without holding the hand of an adult. I had never been on a city street alone without my glasses. I was on the eve of my twenty-seventh birthday when I was stabbed. The last time I had been out in public without my glasses I was not permitted to be awake at 10:24, which is the time it has become at this point in the story.

A figure ran toward me, a man. I was afraid; I stopped. He must have seen my fear, this man, because he waved his hands in the air and shouted, "I'm a good Samaritan! A good Samaritan!" I trusted his words, his biblical reference, and let him lead me to some steps across the street.

From Officer Pitoniak's incident report, composed at 22:24 on August 7, 1994:

> This investigating officer did find one white male subject and one Black female subject on the stairs of an apartment complex located across the street from 24 Whitney Avenue. Both subjects had stab wounds to the stomach areas and Bleeding Profusely. Due to the extent of injuries and calling for medical assistance this officer was not able to obtain any identification of victims.

What's your name? What's your Social Security number? I fired these questions at the white male subject shortly before Officer Pitoniak arrived. The young white man, whom I had never seen before, was sitting on the steps a few feet away from me. He was going into shock, and I was trying to keep him from doing so. I kept up my round of questioning, and he mumbled some answers. "I'm going out, I'm going out," he said, and fainted. It was only then that I really looked at him. He's white as a sheet, I thought. Literally, *white as a sheet*. This is what it looks like, I thought. The young man had pale skin, light-blond hair, and wore a white oxford shirt. The contrast between the blood and his skin, hair, and shirt must have been dramatic, but I don't remember the blood. I watched him. The more he faded away, the less able I was to ignore what was happening just under my hand. An EMT came close to me and asked about the young man, and I answered him. I talked and talked, told my story, posed as a witness, even as I was seeing sparks and hearing static and the EMT's badge started to blur. Trained to recognize the signs of shock, the EMT cradled my head and took my hand away from my side. His gloved hand, like my bare hand, became wet with my blood. He said something to his partner, who was tending to the white male subject. Suddenly, there was a commotion around me. He laid me down carefully on the steps. He held my bloody hand as his team moved me onto a gurney. At some point, our eyes met and we laughed. The more I laughed, the more I came to. The more I laughed, the more my wound gaped open, which made us laugh even harder. It was all so *absurd*.

The same EMT came to visit me in the hospital before I went into surgery. He seemed somber and shaken. Watching him look at me, I realized that my situation was dire. I tried to mirror his grave expression and warned myself that getting stabbed was serious business, but I wanted to laugh with him again. The incident still seemed mostly ridiculous.

Emily Bernard, 26, is listed in serious condition
at Yale-New Haven Hospital. Her birthday is
Thursday.
—from "The Victims," *New Haven Register*,
Tuesday, August 9, 1994

On my birthday, a white couple—a man and a
woman, middle-aged—brought chocolates to my hospital room. "It just seemed so sad that you had to spend your birthday in the hospital," said the woman while her husband looked on sympathetically. I was moved to tears, which was surely a consequence of the morphine as much as the purity of their kindness. The morphine was there to shield me from pain, a consequence of healing, my body reassembling itself. A word about the pain: it didn't hurt, the knife. That and the fact that no one died are the two things I always make sure to say in my version of this story.

I did experience terrible pain on the night of August 7. The person responsible for it was the surgeon on call. I lay on a gurney, feeling helpless and afraid. The surgeon walked over and without saying a word to me, or even looking in my direction, plunged his fingers into my gaping wound. I gasped and instinctively grabbed his hand. It was only then that the man looked at me, and said icily, "Don't. Touch. My. Hand." His eyes were Aryan-blue and as cold as his voice. I asked questions about what was happening and he refused to respond. Only the attending nurses treated me with any kindness or respect. Whenever I tell the story of the night I got stabbed, I always say that the person who did the most injury to me, who left the deepest wounds, was not Daniel Silva, but the surgeon.

If my story is about pain, it's also about rage. Rage is a physical condition, I've learned from this experience. I feel it now, when I recount the story of the doctor and recall his face, voice, and hands.

Sometimes, rage surfaces without warning when I am out in the world. A few months ago, I was walking in downtown New Haven when a young man—presumably a Yale student—suddenly broke into a run. This happens all the time. People run because they're in a hurry to get somewhere; they run to cross the street before the light changes; they run to greet someone they are happy to see, which was the case on this day.

This happens every day. But every time it happens to me, alarms go off my body. Blood rushes to my ears, adrenaline spills through my bloodstream like lighter fluid. My heart pounds, my pulse races, my temple throbs. Fight or flight—I'm ready to *fight;* the machine inside switches into gear. It doesn't make any sense: I'm watching a young brown-skinned man in an argyle sweater and chunky glasses hug a young white woman in a flouncy white skirt. Such a sight would normally fill me with happiness, but my body is nearly bursting with rage. He hugs her tightly and lifts her off the ground. She wiggles her feet, and they laugh. I smile and come down.

But it takes a while for the machine to grind down completely and my body to feel normal again. This reaction on the part of my body always throws me. More than my scar, it reminds me of how much of this story I carry inside of me.

"You never get angry about it," a therapist once said to me during a conversation about the stabbing. I explained to her, as I have explained to many people over the years, that I did not look into the eyes of someone who was really there, that—and I know this sounds odd—it wasn't *personal*. He didn't know me. She cocked her head; she wanted something raw. I wanted to cover up. I remembered a conversation I had with a fellow graduate student at a party a few months after I was released from the hospital.

"Emily, he didn't hurt your . . . lady parts?" she whispered excitedly.

"No." I laughed and pulled my jacket together. At the time I was writing an essay about *Their Eyes Were Watching God,* and I understood then what Janie, the main character, meant when she likened her husband's insults to her body to "talkin' under people's clothes."

It was odd, knowing that an acquaintance, a polite, genteel young black woman, had considered my lady parts. But insofar as any story I have ever heard belongs, in some way, to me, my story belongs to her to recount as she pleases. I cannot dictate how she will use this story any more than I could control the knife that let flow this story in the first place.

John, my husband, knew the story of the stabbing before he knew me, having read an essay about the incident by Bruce Shapiro, who was also stabbed that night. "One Violent Crime" was first published in *The Nation* and then reprinted in *Best American Essays.* I don't know when this came up in the course of our dating, but I remember feeling both a little weirded out and also reassured: weirded out, because it is always peculiar to have people know something intimate about you before they know you; reassured, because it's one less thing about yourself, about your past, that you have to explain.

Even though John was already acquainted with this chapter of my history by the time we met, he has had to sit through numerous renditions I have told over the years. Once, not long after we decided to marry, we were in New York. I had just given a talk to promote my first book. After the talk, we met up with Susan and Brian, who worked at my publishing house, in the bar of the hotel where John and I were staying.

I had recently experienced another bout of recurring abdominal pain occasioned by adhesions, but at the time, I didn't know what adhesions were. Adhesions are, in essence, a complex dance between one's scar tissue and intestines. Since the stabbing, adhesions have sent me back to the hospital three times. The first time, the dance had been gaining in intensity for years without my knowing it. The dancing stopped but the dancers were still intertwined; I could no longer process food. Yet I was vomiting, stream upon stream of thick yellow bile. And the pain—it was like being ripped in two, tissue by tissue; I *was* being ripped in two, no similes necessary. Then, as mysteriously as these episodes began, they simply ended.

Brian knew about the pain I had been experiencing. That night at the bar, he asked me how I was feeling. I said I suspected the abdominal pain had something to do with the stabbing, although no doctor had yet confirmed that, and Susan said, I didn't know you were stabbed, and I said, Oh, you didn't know? And Brian said, You've never told me the whole story. So off I went. I told the story in all of its glory, lingering on the gruesome details. At some point, John got up abruptly and walked away from the table.

Brian looked concerned, but I was sure that John was only going to the bathroom. I turned back to the table and to my story, but Brian kept his eye on John, who suddenly fell backward on the floor of the bar, flat as a domino.

It was remarkable—John falling backward like a tree having met an ax. His head went *thunk* as it hit the marble floor. The lights in the bar came up so swiftly, it was as if God himself had flipped the switch. Brian was suddenly at his side, cradling his head, pelting him with questions like "What's your name?" "What's your Social Security number?" "Who's the president?" Brian and I must have watched the same television crime dramas. John lay on his back on the floor in his suit jacket. His eyes were dazed, straining to register Brian's face and the words coming out of his mouth. It was all that talk of blood, he would tell me later, the blood that I don't remember, the blood that was, according to police reports, all over the walls. Brian said it was the most romantic thing he'd ever witnessed, but I think the fainting had to do with being a man— women, after all, become well acquainted with blood over the course of their lives. At any rate, the story of my stabbing belongs to John, too.

My daughters, Giulia and Isabella, are not products of my body, but they have been careful observers of and frequent travelers across the terrain of their mother's skin for many years. Since they began to talk, they have had questions. Their questions about my scar lead, inevitably, to a knife. What happened, Mommy? A man hurt me, he was sick. Why, Mommy? He was really sick. Like he had a stomachache, Mommy? Yes, a really bad stomachache, but it was in his mind, and he didn't have any medicine. The girls fall silent, worry tight across their foreheads. It will never happen to you, I say, and it will never happen to me again.

Being a parent brings up the question again of what to call this story. Over the years: The incident. The stabbing. *My* stabbing. The accident (what my parents called it). What does Isabella call it? *Your face, Mommy. Your face.*

The girls were two and a half years old when I returned to the hospital in the fall of 2008; it was my second bout of adhesions. It was late at night when John and I finally accepted the fact that I would have to go back to the hospital. We asked a friend to stay with the girls while John took me to the emergency room. I can't know what it was like for my daughters to wake up in the morning and find me gone. Gone I remained for seven days. What sense could this make to a two-year-old? Once I was stable, John brought them to see me in the hospital. What did I look like? Hair wild; eyes glassy from morphine; an IV in my arm; an NG tube in my nose. A nasogastric tube goes through the nose, down the throat, and into the stomach. It is as unpleasant as it sounds and it has saved my life three times now. It was there to decompress my bowel, which was in distress, and it was held in place by several rudimentary pieces of masking tape. It hurt and it looked terrible.

I could tell how bad it looked from Isabella's expression. Giulia, who never takes anything very seriously, who has a "well, that's life" way of approaching the world, hopped right up onto my hospital bed and began fooling around with the call button. Isabella, however, clung to her father, her impossibly big brown eyes even impossibly bigger. She stared at the wild-haired creature and said nothing, shook her head when I held my arms out. She was "fixed to the spot." Even now, when she remembers the hospital, remembers what it was like for her to see me there, what her adolescent mind seizes upon, what she may continue to seize upon for the rest of her life, regardless of her own wishes or mine, what she remembers is captured in a single phrase that she first uttered in her car seat a couple of weeks after I returned home: "Your face, Mommy. Your face."

In 1994, I was stabbed in the gut by a stranger in a coffee shop. I have proof: a scar (puffy and wormlike, over the points of entry and exit); another scar, similar in texture but much longer, that covers the work of two surgeons (so far); it covers the points of entry and exit of their own knives. A midline incision, it's called, and it begins just under my breastbone and ends at my pubic bone, stem to stern, fore to aft. Reminders. Every morning and night. Evidence. I have police and hospital records; newspaper articles; my memories and the memories of others close to me. This happened to me.

I've been telling this story since the night of August 7, 1994. That night, I told this story to doctors, nurses, police officers, family, and friends. Since then, I have related it to gynecologists, dentists, ophthalmologists, general practitioners, a dermatologist, even a podiatrist, and of course, emergency room physicians—all of these men and women in white coats, and their assistants, too. "Have you ever been hospitalized?" reads every single form in every single doctor's waiting room. It's either "yes" or "no." There's no box for "I'd rather not get into it today, thank you very much." So, I tell what happened: in 1994, I was stabbed in the gut by a stranger in a coffee shop. I raise my shirt and reveal my wound. I reassure my listener: it didn't hurt; no one died.

"The fact that she's already telling the story, that's a sign of healing," I heard the doctor tell my mother as I drifted in and out of my morphine haze a few days after I was stabbed. The story that has saved me, though, isn't true. In the story I tell, there isn't much blood; the police reports say otherwise. In my story, I wasn't badly hurt; newspaper accounts and hospital records have me in serious condition. In my story, there is no anger; my body begs to differ. Memory lies. To this day, when I speak of the knife, my mind conjures up a small thin blade, flat and tidy. It is a quick, involuntary association, like Daniel Silva and Gallagher. By chance, several years ago, I saw a hunting knife in a glass cabinet. I got close to the six-inch blade and shook my head, backing away. No. That has nothing to do with *me*.

But, surely, the knife, as well as this story, has everything to do with Daniel Silva, to whom this story also belongs.

Ten years ago, I received an email that included a link to an article from Renee, a friend in New Haven. "Is this you, Emily?" read the subject field. I opened the link:

Daniel Silva, who burned down his house, then stabbed seven people with a knife at a New Haven coffee shop, pleaded guilty to second-degree arson Tuesday and received a suspended 10-year sentence that will allow him to eventually be placed in a halfway house.

During a hearing at Superior Court in Waterbury, Silva, now 53, apologized to the stabbing victims and said he was not in a rational "state of mind" on that day in August 1994. Senior Assistant State's Attorney Gary Nicholson told Judge Richard Damiani that the state recommended the plea arrangement, which includes five years of probation and a list of conditions, because Silva has been confined at Connecticut Valley Hospital since the assaults and arson.

Nicholson noted Silva had been repeatedly ruled incompetent to stand trial for the assaults. Those first-degree assault charges were dismissed in 2000 because, under state law, a defendant facing such charges must be restored to competency within five years. No such limitation applies to first-degree arson. Last month, Silva was ruled competent to stand trial on the arson charges, based on testimony from an assistant clinical professor at Yale School of Medicine who interviewed him . . .

Silva, dressed in a coat and tie, is bearded and balding. He rose and told Damiani, "I apologize to the court and to the people that were hurt. I never meant to do what I did. If I hadn't been in that state of mind, it never would have occurred."

—*New Haven Register,* September 9, 2009

Yes, Renee. It's me.

Teaching the N-Word

Once riding in old Baltimore,
Heart-filled, head-filled with glee,
I saw a Baltimorean
Keep looking straight at me.

Now I was eight and very small,
And he was no whit bigger,
And so I smiled, but he poked out
His tongue, and called me, "Nigger."

I saw the whole of Baltimore
From May until December;
Of all the things that happened there
That's all that I remember.

—COUNTEE CULLEN, "Incident" (1925)

OCTOBER 2004

Eric is crazy about queer theory. I think it is safe to say that Eve Sedgwick, Judith Butler, and Lee Edelman have changed his life. Every week, he comes to my office to report on the connections he is making between the works of these writers and the books he is reading for the class he is taking with me, African American Autobiography.

I like Eric. So tonight, even though it is well after six and I am eager to go home, I keep our conversation going. I ask him what he thinks about the word "queer," whether or not he believes, independent of the theorists he admires, that epithets can ever really be reclaimed and reinvented.

"'Queer' has important connotations for me," he says. "It's daring, political. I embrace it." He folds his arms across his chest and then unfolds them.

I am suspicious.

"What about 'nigger'?" I ask. "If we're talking about the importance of transforming hateful language, what about that word?" From my bookshelf, I pull down Randall Kennedy's book *Nigger: The Strange Career of a Troublesome Word* and turn it back so its cover faces Eric. "Nigger," in stark white type against a black background, is staring at him, staring at anyone who happens to be walking past the open door behind him.

Over the next thirty minutes or so, Eric and I talk about "nigger." He is uncomfortable; every time he says "nigger," he drops his voice and does not meet my eyes. I know that he does not want to say the word; he is following my lead. He does not want to say it because he is white; he does not want to say it because I am black. I feel my power as his professor, the mentor he has so ardently adopted. I feel the power of Randall Kennedy's book in my hands, its title crude and unambiguous. *Say it*, we both instruct this white student. And he does.

It is late. No one moves through the hallway. I think about my colleagues, some of whom still sit at their own desks. At any minute, they might pass my office on their way out of the building. What would they make of this scene? Most of my colleagues are white. What would I think if I walked by an office and saw one of them holding up *Nigger* to a white student's face? A black student's face?

"I think I am going to add 'Who Can Say "Nigger"?' to our reading for next week," I say to Eric. "It's an article by Kennedy that covers some of the ideas in this book." I tap *Nigger* with my finger and then put it down on my desk.

"I really wish there was a black student in our class," Eric says, as he gathers his books to leave.

As usual, I have assigned way too much reading. Even though we begin class discussion with references to the three essays required for today, our conversation drifts quickly to "Who Can Say 'Nigger'?" and plants itself there. We talk about the word, who can say it, who won't say it, who wants to say it, and why. There are eleven students in the class. All of them are white.

Our class discussion is lively and intense; everyone seems impatient to speak. We talk about language, history, and identity. Most students say "the n-word" instead of "nigger." Only one or two students actually use the word in their comments. When they do, they use the phrase "the word 'nigger,'" as if to cushion it. Sometimes they make quotation marks with their fingers. I notice Lauren looking around. Finally she raises her hand.

"I have a question; it's somewhat personal. I don't want to put you on the spot."

"Go ahead, Lauren," I say with relief.

"Okay, so how does it feel for you to hear us say that word?"

I have an answer ready.

"I don't enjoy hearing it. But I don't think that I feel more offended by it than you do. What I mean is, I don't think I have a special place of pain inside of me that the word touches because I am black." *We are both human beings,* I am trying to say. She nods her head, seemingly satisfied. Even inspired, I hope.

I am lying, of course.

I am grateful to Lauren for acknowledging my humanity in our discussion. But I do not want me—my feelings, my experiences, my humanity—to become the center of classroom discussion. Here at the University of Vermont, I routinely teach classrooms full of white students. I want to educate them, transform them. I want to teach them things about race they will never forget. To achieve this, I believe I must give of myself. I want to give to them—but I want to keep much of myself to myself. How much? I have a new answer to this question every week.

I always give my students a lecture at the beginning of every African American studies course I teach. I tell them, in essence, not to confuse my body with the body of the book. I tell them that while it would be disingenuous for me to suggest that my own racial identity has nothing to do with my love for African American literature, my race is only one of the many reasons why I stand before them. "I stand here," I say, "because I have a PhD, just like all your other professors." I make sure to tell them that my PhD, like my BA, comes from Yale.

"In order to get this PhD," I continue, "I studied with some of this country's foremost authorities on African American literature, and a significant number of these people are white.

"I say this to suggest that if you fail to fully appreciate this material, it is a matter of your intellectual laziness, not your race. If you cannot grasp the significance of Frederick Douglass's plight, for instance, you are not trying hard enough, and I will not accept that."

I have another part of this lecture. It goes: "Conversely, this material is not the exclusive property of students of color. This is literature. While these books will speak to us emotionally according to our different experiences, none of us is especially equipped to appreciate the intellectual and aesthetic complexities that characterize African American literature. This is American literature, American experience, after all."

Sometimes I give this part of my lecture, but not always. Sometimes I give it and then regret it later.

As soon as Lauren asks me how I feel, it is as if the walls of the room soften and collapse slightly, nudging us a little bit closer together. Suddenly, eleven pairs of eyes are beaming sweet messages at me. I want to laugh. I do. "Look at you all, leaning in," I say. "How close we have all become."

I sit at the end of a long narrow table. Lauren usually sits at the other end. The rest of the students flank us on either side. When I make my joke, a few students, all straight men, I notice, abruptly pull themselves back. They shift their eyes away from me, looking instead at their notebooks, the table. I have made them ashamed to show that they care about me, I realize. They are following the cues I have been giving them since the beginning of the semester, cues that they should take this class seriously, that I will be offended if they do not. "African American studies has had to struggle to exist at all," I have said. "You owe it your respect." *Don't be too familiar,* is what I am really saying. *Don't be too familiar with me.*

Immediately, I regret having made a joke of their sincere attempt to offer me their care. They want to know me; they see this moment as an opportunity. But I can't stop. I make more jokes, mostly about them, and what they are saying and not saying. I can't seem to help myself.

Eric, who is sitting near me, does not recoil at my jokes; he does not respond to my not-so-subtle efforts to push him and everyone else back. He continues to lean in, his torso flat against the table. He looks at me. He raises his hand.

"Emily," he says, "would you tell them what you told me the other day in your office? You were talking about how you dress and what it means to you."

"Yes," I begin slowly. "I was telling Eric about how important it is to me that I come to class dressed up."

"And remember what you said about Todd? You said that Todd exercises his white privilege by dressing so casually for class."

Todd is one of my closest friends in the English department. His office is next door to mine. I don't remember talking about Todd's clothing habits with Eric, but I must have. I struggle to come up with a comfortably vague response to stop Eric's prodding. My face grows hot. Everyone is waiting.

"Well, I don't know if I put it exactly like that, but I do believe that Todd's style of dress reflects his ability to move in the world here—everywhere, really—less self-consciously than I do." As I sit here, I grow increasingly more alarmed at what I am revealing: my personal philosophies; my attitudes about my friend's style of dress; my insecurities; my feelings. I quietly will Eric to stop, even as I am impressed by his determination. I meet his eyes again.

"And you. You were saying that the way you dress, it means something, too," Eric says. *On with this tug of war,* I think.

I relent, let go of the rope. "Listen, I will say this. I am aware that you guys, all of my students at UVM, have very few black professors. I am aware, in fact, that I may be the first black teacher many of you have ever had. And the way I dress for class reflects my awareness of that possibility." I look sharply at Eric. *That's it. No more.*

SEPTEMBER 2004

On the first day of class, Nate asks me what I want to be called.

"Oh, I don't know," I say, fussing with equipment in the room. I know. But I feel embarrassed, as if I have been found out. "What do you think?" I ask them.

They shuffle around, equally embarrassed. We all know that I have to decide, and that whatever I decide will shape our classroom dynamic in very important ways.

"What does Gennari ask you to call him?" I have inherited several of these students from my husband, John Gennari, another professor of African American studies. He is white.

"Oh, we call him John," Nate says with confidence. I am immediately envious of the easy warmth he seems to feel for John. I suspect it has to do with the name thing.

"Just call me Emily, then. This is an honors class, after all. And I do know several of you already. And then wouldn't it be strange to call the husband 'John' and the wife 'Professor'?" Okay, I have convinced myself.

Nate says, "Well, John and I play basketball in a pickup game on Wednesdays. So, you know, it would be weird for me to be checking him and calling him Professor Gennari."

We all laugh and move on to other topics. But my mind locks onto an image of my husband and Nate on the basketball court, two white men covered in sweat, body to body, heads down, focused on the ball.

OCTOBER 2004

"It's not that I can't say it, it's that I don't want to. I will not say it," Sarah says. She wears her copper-red hair in a short, smart style that makes her look older than her years. When she smiles I remember how young she is. She is not smiling now. She looks indignant. She is indignant because I am insinuating that there is a problem with the fact that no one in the class will say "nigger." Her indignation pleases me.

Good.

"I'd just like to remind you all that just because a person refuses to say 'nigger,' that doesn't mean that person is not a racist," I say. They seem to consider this.

"And another thing," Sarah continues. "About dressing for class? I dislike it when my professors come to class in shorts, for instance. This is a profession. They should dress professionally."

Later, I tell John about our class discussion. When I get to Sarah's comment about professors in shorts, he says, "Good for her."

I hold up *Nigger* and show its cover to the class. I hand it to the person on my left and gesture for him to pass the book around the room.

"Isn't it strange that when we refer to this book, we keep calling it 'the n-word'?"

Lauren comments on the effect of one student who actually said it. "Colin looked like he was being strangled." Of the effect on the other students, she says, "I saw us all collectively cringing."

"Would you be able to say it if I weren't here?" I blurt. A few students shake their heads. Tyler's hand shoots up. He always sits directly to my right.

"That's just bullshit," he says to the class, and I force myself not to raise an eyebrow at "bullshit." "If Emily weren't here, you all would be able to say that word."

I note that he himself has not said it, but I do not make this observation out loud.

"No." Sarah is firm. "I just don't want to be the kind of person who says that word, period."

"Even in this context?" I ask.

"Regardless of context," Sarah says.

"Even when it's the title of a book?"

I tell my students that I often work with a book called *Nigger Heaven,* written in 1926 by a white man, Carl Van Vechten.

"Look, I don't want to give you the impression that I am somehow longing for you guys to say 'nigger,'" I tell them, "but I do think that something is lost when you don't articulate it, especially if the context demands its articulation."

"What do you mean? What exactly is lost?" Sarah insists.

"I don't know," I say. I *do* know. But right here, in this moment, the last thing I want is to win an argument that winds up with Sarah saying "nigger" out loud.

Throughout our discussion, Nate is the only student who will say "nigger" out loud. He sports a shearling coat and a Caesar haircut. He quotes Jay-Z. He makes a case for "nigga." He is that kind of white kid; he is down. "He is so down, he's almost up," Todd will say in December, when I show him the title page of Nate's final paper for this class. The page contains one word, "Nigger," in black type against a white background. It is an autobiographical essay. It is a very good paper.

OCTOBER 1994

Nate reminds me of a student in the very first class I taught all on my own, a senior seminar called Race and Representation. *Pulp Fiction* had just come out. I spent an entire three-hour class session arguing with my students over the way race was represented in the movie. One student in particular passionately resisted my attempts to analyze the way Tarantino used "nigger" in the film.

"What is his investment in this word? What is he, as a

white director, getting out of saying 'nigger' over and over again?" I asked.

After some protracted verbal arm wrestling, the student gave in.

"Okay, okay! I want to be the white guy who can say 'nigger' to black guys and get away with it. I want to be the cool white guy who can say 'nigger.'"

"Thank you! Thank you for admitting it!" I said, and everyone laughed.

He was tall. He wore tie-dyed T-shirts and had messy, curly brown hair. I don't remember his name.

After *Pulp Fiction* came out, I wrote my brother James an earnest, academic email. I wanted to "initiate a dialogue" with him about the "cultural and political implications of the various usages of 'nigger' in popular culture."

His one-sentence reply went something like this: "Nigga, niggoo, niggu, negreaux, negrette, niggrum."

"Do you guys ever read *The Source* magazine?" In 1994 my students knew about *The Source;* some of them had read James's monthly column.

"He's my brother," I said, not bothering to mask my pride. "He's coming to visit class in a couple of weeks, when we discuss hip-hop culture."

The eyes of the tie-dyed student glistened.

"Quentin Tarantino is a cool-ass white boy!" James said on the day he came to visit my class. "He is one cool white boy."

My students clapped and laughed.

"That's what I said." My tie-dyed student sighed.

James looked at me slyly. I narrowed my eyes at him. *Thanks a lot.*

SEPTEMBER 2004

Several months ago, I was waiting to cross Main Street in order to get to my office after class. It was late April, near the end of the semester, and it seemed as if everyone was outside. Parents were visiting, and students were yelling to one another, introducing family members from across the street. Everyone was giddy with the promise of spring, which always comes so late in Vermont, if it comes at all. People smiled at me—wide, grinning smiles. I smiled back. At the same time I tried to steady the thrumming of my heart by breathing deeply and repeating to myself, *You are safe. You are safe.*

Traffic was heavy. A car was stopped near me; I heard rough male voices. Out of the corner of my eye, I looked into the car: all white. I looked away, but I could feel the men surveying the small crowd that was carrying me along. As traffic picked up again, one of the men yelled out, "Queers! Fags!" There was laughter. Then the car roared off.

I was stunned. I stopped walking and let the words wash over me. *Queer. Fag.* I remembered my role as a teacher, a mentor, in loco parentis, even though there were real parents everywhere. I looked around to check for the wounds caused by those hateful words. I peered down the street: too late for a license plate. All around me, students and parents marched to their destinations. *Didn't you hear that?* I wanted to shout.

All the while I was thinking, *Not nigger. Not yet.*

OCTOBER 2004

Nate jumps in.

"Don't you grant a word power by not saying it? Aren't we in some way amplifying its ugliness by avoiding it?" he asks.

"I am afraid of how I will be affected by saying it," Lauren says. "I just don't want that word in my mouth."

Tyler remembers a phrase attributed to the writer Farai Chideya in Randall Kennedy's essay. He finds it and reads it to us. "She says that the n-word is the 'trump card, the nuclear bomb of racial epithets.'"

"Do you agree with that?" I ask.

Eleven heads nod vigorously.

"Nuclear bombs annihilate. What do you imagine will be destroyed if you guys use the word in here?"

Shyly, they look at me, all of them, and I understand. Me. It is my annihilation they imagine.

NOVEMBER 2004

Some of My Best Friends, my anthology of essays about interracial friendship, came out in August, and the publicity department has arranged for various interviews and other promotional events. When I did an on-air interview on a New York radio show, one of the hosts, Janice, a black woman, told me that the reason she could not marry a white man was because she believed if things ever got heated between them, the white man would call her a nigger.

I nodded my head. I had heard this reasoning before. But strangely I had all but forgotten it. The fact that I had forgotten to fear "nigger" coming from the mouth of my white husband was more interesting to me than her fear, alive and ever-present.

"Are you biracial?"

"No."

"Are you married to a white man?"

"Yes."

These were among the first words exchanged between Janice and me. I could tell—by the way she looked at me, and didn't look at me; by the way she kept her body turned away from me; by her tone—that she had made up her mind about me before I entered the room. I could tell that she didn't like what she had decided about me, and that she had decided I was the wrong kind of black person. Maybe it was what I had written in *Some of My Best Friends*. Maybe it was the fact that I had decided to edit a collection about interracial friendship at all. When we met, she said, "I don't trust white people," as decisively and exactly as if she were handing me her business card. I knew she was telling me that I was foolish to trust them, to marry one. I was relieved to look inside myself and see that I was okay, I was still standing. A few years before, her silent judgment—this silent judgment from any black person—would have crushed me.

When she said that she could "tell" I was married to a white man, I asked her how. She said, "Because you are so friendly" and did a little dance with her shoulders. I laughed.

But Janice couldn't help it; she liked me in spite of herself. As the interview progressed, she let the corners of her mouth turn up into a smile. She admitted that she had a few white friends, even if they sometimes drove her crazy. At a commercial break, she said, "Maybe I ought to try a white man." She was teasing me, of course. She hadn't changed her mind about white people, or dating a white man, but she had changed her mind about me. It mattered to me. I took what she was offering. But when the interview was over, I left it behind, along with the microphone and sound effects and "words from our sponsor."

John thought my story about the interview was hilarious. When I got home, he listened to the tape they gave me at the station. He said he wanted to use the interview in one of his classes.

A few days later, I told him what Janice said about dating a white man, that she won't because she is afraid he will call her a nigger. As I told him, I felt an unfamiliar shyness creep up on me.

"That's just so far out of . . . it's not in my head at all." He was having difficulty coming up with the words he wanted, I could tell. But that was okay. I knew what he meant. I looked at him sitting in his chair, the chair his mother gave us. I can usually find him in that chair when I come home. He is John, I told myself. And he is white. No more or less John, and no more or less white, than he was before the interview, and Janice's reminder of the fear I had forgotten to feel.

I tell my students in African American Autobiography about Janice. "You would not believe the indignities I have suffered in my humble attempts to 'move this product,' as they say in publishing," I say. "I have been surrounded by morons, and now I gratefully return to the land of the intellectually agile." They laugh.

I flatter them, in part because I feel guilty that I have missed so many classes in order to do publicity for my book. But I cringe, thinking of how I have called Janice, another black woman, a "moron" in front of these white students. I do not tell my students she is black.

"Here is a story for your students," John says. We are in the car, on our way to Cambridge for the weekend to visit friends. "The only time I ever heard 'nigger' in my home growing up was when my father's cousin was over for a visit. It was 1988, I remember. Jesse Jackson was running for president. My father's cousin was sitting in the kitchen, talking to my parents about the election. 'I'm going to vote for the nigger,' my father's cousin said. 'He's the only one who cares about the working man.'"

John laughs. He often laughs when he hears something extraordinary, whether it's good or bad.

"That's fascinating," I say.

The next time the class meets, I tell my students this story.

"So what do we care about in this story?" I say. "The fact that John's father's cousin used a racial epithet, or the fact that his voting for Jackson conveys a kind of ultimate respect for him? Isn't his voting for Jackson more important for black progress than how his father's cousin *feels*?"

I don't remember what the students said. What I

remember is that I tried to project for them a sense that I was untroubled by saying "nigger," by my husband's saying "nigger," by his father's cousin's having said "nigger," by his parents'—my in-laws'—tolerance of "nigger" in their home, years ago, before I came along. What I remember is that I leaned on the word "feels" with a near sneer in my voice. *It's an intellectual issue,* I said, beaming at them, and then I directed it back at myself. *It has nothing to do with how it makes me feel.*

After my interview with Janice, I look at the white people around me differently, as if from a distance. I do this, from time to time, almost as an exercise. I even do it to my friends, particularly my friends. Which one of them has "nigger" in the back of her throat?

I go out for drinks with David, my senior colleague. It is our weekly ritual. We go out on Thursdays after class, and we always go to the same place. I know that he will order, in succession, two draft beers, and that he will ask the waitress to help him choose the second. "What do you have on draft that is interesting tonight?" he will say. I order red wine, and I, too, always ask the waitress's advice. Then we order a selection of cheeses, again soliciting assistance. We have our favorite waitresses. We like the ones who indulge us.

Tonight David orders a cosmopolitan.

We never say it, but I suspect we both like the waitresses who appreciate the odd figure we cut. He is white, sixty-something, male. I am black, thirty-something, female. Not such an odd pairing elsewhere, but uncommon in Burlington, insofar as black people are uncommon in Burlington.

Something you can't see is that we are both from the South. Different Souths, perhaps, thirty years apart, black and white. I am often surprised by how much I like his company. *All the way up here,* I sometimes think when I am with him, *and I am sitting with the South, the white South that, all of my childhood, I longed to escape.* I once had a white boyfriend from New Orleans. "A white southerner, Emily?" my mother asked, and sighed with worry. I understood. We broke up.

David and I catch up. We talk about the writing we have been doing. We talk each other out of bad feelings we are harboring against this and that person. (Like most southerners, like the South in general, David and I have long memories.) We talk about classes. I describe to him the conversation I have been having with my students about "nigger." He laughs at my anecdotes.

I am on my second glass of wine. I try to remember to keep my voice down. It's a very nice restaurant. *People in Burlington do not want to hear "nigger" while they are eating a nice dinner,* I think, chastising myself. I am tipsy.

As we leave, I accidentally knock my leg against a chair. *You are drunk,* I tell myself. *You are drunk and black in a restaurant in Burlington, Vermont. What were you thinking?* I feel eyes on me as I walk out of the restaurant, eyes that may have been focused elsewhere, as far as I know, because I do not allow myself to look.

Later that evening, I am alone. I remember that David recently gave me a poem of his to read, a poem about his racist grandmother, now dead, whom he remembers using the word "nigger" often and with relish. I lie in bed and reconstruct the scene of David and me in the restaurant and our conversation about "nigger." Was his grandmother at the table with us all along?

The next day, I see David in his office, which is next to mine, on the other side from Todd. I knock on the door. He invites me in. I sit in the chair I always sit in when I come to talk to him. He tells me how much he enjoyed our conversation the night before.

"Me, too," I say. "But today it's as if I'm looking at you from across something. It has to do with race." I blame a book I am reading, a book for African American Autobiography, *The Black Notebooks* by Toi Derricotte.

"Have you read it?" David is a poet, like Derricotte.

"No, but I know Toi and enjoy her poetry. Everything I know about her work would lead me to believe that I would enjoy that book." He leans back in his chair, his arms folded behind his head.

"Well, it's making me think about things, remember the ways that you and I will always be different," I say abruptly.

"I hope not." He laughs and looks puzzled.

"It's probably just temporary." I don't ask him my question about his grandmother, whether or not she is always somewhere with him, in him, in the back of his throat.

John is at an African American studies conference in New York. Usually I am thrilled to have the house to myself for a few days. But this time, I mope. I sit at the dining room table, write this essay, and gaze out the window.

A few hours later, he calls and describes the activity at the conference. He tells me delicious and predictable gossip about people we know and divas we know of. The personalities, the infighting—greedily we sift over details on the phone.

"Did you enjoy your evening with David last night?" he asks.

"I did, very much," I say. "But give me more of the who-said-what." I know he's in a hurry. In fact, he's talking on a cell phone (my cell phone; he refuses to get one of his own) as he walks down the street.

"Oh, you know these Negroes." His voice jounces as he walks.

"Yeah," I say, laughing. I wonder who else can hear him.

Todd is married to Hilary, another close friend in the department. She is white. Like John, Todd is out of town this weekend. Since their two boys were born, our godsons, John and I see them less frequently than we used to. But Hilary and I are determined to spend some time together this weekend, with our husbands away.

Burlington traffic keeps me from her and the boys for an hour even though she lives only blocks away from me. When I get there, the boys are ready for their baths, one more feeding, and then bed. Finally, they are down, and we settle into grown-up conversation. I tell her about my class, our discussions about "nigger," and my worries about David.

"That's the thing about the South," Hilary says. I agree,

but then start to wonder about her grandmother. I decided I do not want to know, not tonight.

I tell her about the incident with the men in the car and their hateful words. I confess that the reason I don't like to cross Main Street is due to a persistent fear that something like that might happen.

"Did you grow up hearing that?" she asks. Even though we are close, and alone, she does not say the word.

I start to tell her a story I have never told anyone. It is a story about the only time I remember being called a nigger to my face.

"I was a teenager, maybe sixteen. I was standing on a sidewalk, trying to cross a busy street after school to meet some friends. I happened to make eye contact with a white man in a car that was stopped in traffic. Anyway, he just kind of said it, kind of spit it up at me.

"Oh, that's why," I say, stunned. She looks at me, just as surprised.

DECEMBER 2004

I am walking down a Burlington street with my friend Anh. My former quilting teacher, Anh is several years younger than I am. She has lived in Vermont her whole life. She is Vietnamese; her parents are white. Early in our friendship, she told me her father was a logger, as were most of the men in her family. *Generations of Vietnamese loggers in Vermont,* I mused. It wasn't until I started to describe her to someone else that I realized she must be adopted.

Anh and I commiserate often about being minorities

in Burlington, but we usually do it silently. In quilting class, we would give each other looks that said, *You are not alone* or *Oh, brother* when the subject of race came up in our class, which consisted entirely of white women, aside from the two of us.

There was the time, for instance, when one of her students explained why black men found her so attractive. "I have a black girl's butt," she said. Anh and I gave each other the *Oh, brother* look, then bent our heads back over our sewing machines.

As we walk, I tell her about African American Autobiography and the discussion my students and I have been having about "nigger." She listens and then describes to me the latest development in her on-again, off-again relationship with her boyfriend, a scuba instructor.

"He says everything has changed," she tells me. "He's going to clean up the messes in his life." She laughs.

Once, Anh introduced me to the boyfriend she had before the scuba instructor when I ran into them at a restaurant. Like the scuba instructor, he is white.

"I've heard a lot about you," I said, and put out my hand.

"I've never slept with a black woman," he said, and shook my hand. There was wonder in his voice. I excused myself and went back to my table. Later, when I looked over at them, they were sitting side by side and not speaking.

Even though Anh and I exchanged our usual glances that night, I doubted we would be able to recover our growing friendship. *Who could she be, dating someone like that?* The next time I heard from her, she had broken up with him.

I am rooting for the scuba instructor.

"He told me he's a new person," she says.

"Well, what did you say?" I ask her.

"In the immortal words of Jay-Z, I told him, 'Nigga, please.'"

We laugh hard for the next two blocks.

In lieu of a final class, my students come over for dinner. One by one, they file in. John takes coats while I pretend to look for things in the refrigerator. I can't stop smiling.

"The Books of Your Life" is the topic for tonight. I have asked them to bring a book, a poem, a passage, any kind of art that has affected them. Hazel has brought a children's book. Tyler describes the television show *Saved by the Bell*. Nate talks about Freud. Dave has brought a photograph. Eric reads "The Seacoast of Despair" from *Slouching Toward Bethlehem* by Joan Didion.

I read from *Annie John* by Jamaica Kincaid. Later I will wonder why I did not read "Incident" by Countee Cullen, the poem that has been circulating in my head ever since we began our discussion about "nigger." *What held me back from bringing "Incident" to class?* The question will stay with me for months.

The night of our dinner is an emotional one. I tell them that they are the kind of students a professor dreams about. They give me a gift certificate to the restaurant that David and I frequent. I give them copies of *Some of My Best Friends* and inscribe each one. Eric demands a hug, and then they all do. I happily comply. We talk about meeting again as a class, maybe once or twice in the spring. Two students who are going abroad promise to keep in touch through our listserv, which we all agree to keep active until the end of the academic year, at least. After they leave, the house is quiet and empty.

Weeks later, I post "Incident" on our listserv and ask them to respond with their reactions. Weeks of silence go by. After some prodding, Lauren posts an analysis of the poem, and then her personal reactions to it. I thank her online and ask for more responses. More silence.

I get emails and visits from these students about other matters, some of them race related. Eric still comes by my office regularly. Once he brings his mother to meet me, a kind and engaging woman who gives me a redolent candle she purchased in France. She tells me her son enjoyed African American Autobiography. Eric and I smile at each other.

A few days later, I see Eric outside the campus bookstore.

"What did you think about 'Incident'?" I ask him.

"I've been meaning to write you about it. I promise I will."

In the meantime, *Nigger* is back in its special place on my office bookshelf. It is tucked away so that only I can see the title on its spine, and then only with some effort.

Interstates

I.

John, my parents, and I are heading south on Route 55 from Nashville to Hazlehurst, Mississippi. He is driving; my father rides shotgun. I sit in the back with my mother, holding my breath. The entire car is silent, all four of us as still as stones.

"We have to pull over," John says.

It is a midmorning in July. I try to focus on passing cars.

"There's a gas station a few miles up," my father says evenly. He shifts in his seat.

The front left tire is flat.

John and I have been engaged for several months at this point in my life story. This is not his first visit to Nashville, but it is his first trip to Mississippi, where he will meet my extended family—my mother's mother, sisters, cousins, and nieces.

The car belongs to my father, who has entrusted the wheel to John as a symbol of his acquiescence to the new order of things, namely John's having supplanted him as the Man in My Life. But it was only a gesture. When he gave John control of the car, my father did not anticipate that John would actually exercise the authority to take us on a new course. But he does. He pulls over, right there on the shoulder of the interstate, somewhere between Memphis and Jackson. Within minutes John is underneath the car while my parents and I stand in a grassy depression near him. I feel pride as I watch my fiancé's strong, tan arms move in confident, rhythmic silence as he replaces the spent tire with a spare that is, distressingly, nearly flat itself. And I ache for my father, who shifts quickly from side to side, wordlessly hurrying John. There we stand—my black family, as vulnerable as an open window. We are bound by history and helplessness. I focus on John, willing his whiteness and masculine strength toward us, imagining these qualities shielding us from harm, like armor.

The eyes of white men in jeans and work boots travel from John to me to my parents when we arrive at the nearest gas station, which is not the one my father mentioned. He and my mother stay in the car while John, dirty and sweaty, strides into the store. I follow him, carrying a small, impractical purse and decked out in oversized sunglasses. We buy water, fill the tank, and then we're back on the road.

My mother, in a voice sugared with amusement and pride, will tell this story to many people for many years to come. It is a story about how a black family used to do things one way, and then a brand-new white man came into their lives and nothing was ever the same.

2.

My father is a creature of habit, someone who holds tradition in high regard. The reason for his reluctance to stop before we reached the gas station, however, had nothing to do with habit or tradition. Instead it had to do with history, both small and large. His preferred gas station had proven to be a hospitable place over the years. Several times he had received service there without incident, something no black person traveling through the South has ever taken for granted.

When my father arrived in Nashville to attend Fisk University in the 1950s, a black body had to travel along known routes, relying upon the experiences of other black people. For many years, a guide called *The Green Book* informed black travelers of places where it was possible for them to sleep and eat. It was a map of a modern underground railroad. Black bodies out of place would likely encounter insults to their dignity, or worse. *The Green Book* ceased publication in 1966, but to this day, there are cities and towns in this country in which the perils inherent in traveling black have not subsided.

John was not ignorant of the root of my father's anxiety. But the danger presented by the flat tire took precedence over any other type of danger. Somewhere between the clarity of his focus and the complexity of my father's anxiety, perhaps, lies the difference between living white and living black in America. That there is a difference is indisputable; how deep the difference runs is impossible to ascertain. I see the difference. Mostly, I despise it. But my belief that difference can engender pleasure as well as pain made it possible for me to marry a white man.

3.

Before the day of the flat tire, the pattern of this trip had never changed. My mother, brothers, and I always stopped at the same rest stops and gas stations. We always left before dawn in order to reach Memphis, where we had breakfast with my mother's aunt and her family, by midmorning. I had my own routines. I would spend weeks before the trip stockpiling enough books and magazines to last me through the eight-hour ride to Hazlehurst, and then through the long, hot days of visiting relatives. On the first leg, it was so dark in the car that I read by street lamps until fatigue weighed my eyes shut. After breakfast in Memphis, four hours of driving remained. I read and read until my fantasy life beckoned, at which point I hugged my reading material to my chest and daydreamed my way to Mississippi.

When I was a child, my reveries concerned the present: friends, toys, and animals that intrigued me. As an adolescent, I fantasized about the future: what kind of career I would have, where I would live and, most of all, whom I would marry.

Like many fathers, perhaps, mine expected his daughter to bring home someone who looked like him. At some point, however, he must have realized that, since my entire social world was white, there was little chance of this. His concession to this fact must have happened after he sat me down in high school and suggested that I attend Spelman so that I could find a nice Morehouse College man to marry. My mother knew her husband and predicted what he would say to me. "Just keep your mouth closed," she instructed me privately before sending me to the dining room table, where my father waited to dispense his advice.

"White boys only want one thing from black girls," my father warned me when I was an adolescent. He didn't have to explain. I knew what he meant, and understood that he was only trying to protect me from a history that had long preceded me. White exploitation of black female bodies was once a staple feature of life in the American South. I knew the story of my mother's mother, who, as a young woman, had barely escaped the predation of white boys in a pickup truck as she and a few friends walked home one night from a long day of work. The night was black as pitch, the path in front of them barely illuminated by faint lights from houses separated by acres of fields from the road. As the truck crept past, my grandmother could see the pale, hungry faces peering at them from the open window.

"If that truck turns around, let's split up and run to the fields," she told her friends. As if on cue, the headlights reappeared. The women ran and crouched, their hearts beating fast, praying and waiting as the rumble of the engine faded and the truck disappeared into the night.

I shuddered when I imagined my magnificent grandmother scared and running through a field to escape assault at the hands of those white men. While the image moved me terribly, my father's words did not.

By the time I reached high school, my father and I had been at odds for several years. There were no neutral topics. In particular, he objected to the nascent feminism I was cultivating. Once, after church, he found me in a conversation with a peer of his, another doctor, a middle-aged black woman.

"Men are intimidated by strong women," said Dr. Jones just as my father appeared. Sometimes I found Dr. Jones abrasive and patronizing, but in that moment, I was thrilled to be taken seriously by this professional woman, so I nodded vigorously, even though my own experience in the world of romance was limited.

"It's time to go," my father said as he pulled me by the elbow toward the door.

"You know, the reason why Dr. Jones isn't married is because men don't like her personality," he told me on the ride home. "I don't want you spending time around women like that."

At this point in time, it was clear that my father wasn't crazy about my personality either. I was mouthy and rude, he complained to my mother. He admonished me often for talking back. As he continued to disparage Dr. Jones, I kept my mouth closed and resolved to make a point of spending time around her and other women like that as often as possible. Defying him was my mission, much more urgent than my feelings about the doctor, and even more compelling than protecting myself from white boys with bad intentions.

Most of all, I didn't want to be a consequence of history; I wanted to invent my own story. That was before I understood that the drive to create a new story for oneself is the oldest black story there is.

Invent my own stories I did on the long car ride between Nashville and Hazlehurst. Among my reading material were teen magazines with pullout posters of heartthrobs, like white teen idol Leif Garrett. In one, he stood against a wall, dreamy, moppy-haired, and half nude in a slick black shirt unbuttoned to his navel. I mounted the poster on my bedroom wall, right next to a picture of the Swedish tennis star Björn Borg I had ripped out of one of my father's issues of *Sports Illustrated.*

There were black men among my trophies, too, like El DeBarge, the crooner whose "Love Me in a Special Way" I listened to over and over through padded headphones while lying on my back next to the stereo. Jim Rice of the Boston Red Sox looked like Adonis, staring into the out-field, his bat slung over his shoulder in a picture I found in *Time* magazine.

It was never about the bodies. It was the dream of something else, another life, far away from Nashville, the foreign country of men—women, too—where conversations were heavy and sophisticated but unburdened by any talk about race.

4.

John is hungry. As we enter my grandmother's house he looks expectantly at the table in the dining room. Aside from a bowl of fruit, the table is barren. Much else distracts him, however, as he makes his way down a receiving line of the women in the clan to which I belong. My grand-mother, delighted by the simple novelty of his presence, pulls him in for a hug. The joy in the room is palpable and satiating, at least for me; John is looking for a more practi-cal kind of nourishment.

The language of food is John's mother tongue. An Italian American, he grew up in his parents' kitchen, where the proper texture of homemade pasta was the topic of robust controversy. At their dinner table, stories of past meals were remembered in aching, enchanting detail. They lived in the Berkshires but traveled to New Jersey for their cheese. Friends and relatives made pilgrimages to enjoy the spectacle of bounty that was their garden.

John has eaten commercial spaghetti sauce only once. He talks about the incident the way other people shudder at memories of nasty car accidents. He doesn't care for the concept of the potluck; I suspect he secretly believes it was conceived for lazy people. Some of his closest friendships are based exclusively on mutual culinary passions. When I met him, dinner for me consisted of tuna fish I ate out of the can, standing by the sink, more often than I care to recount.

Everyone who knows him has a food story about John. My mother never forgot the first time he ate at her table. She served a slow-cooked pot roast, dripping with gravy, yams dressed with honey and lemon, and bright, buttery sautéed green beans. John also remembers that meal. I don't.

He appreciated the flavor, color, and texture of the food, but even more, he understood the love and labor involved in its preparation. He saw that my mother was offering him a glimpse into her world, who she had been and who she was now. As much his mother's protégé as her son, John understood the dynamic between women and kitchens, maternal sacrifice and sweat. Beneath his words of praise for my mother and her demure reception, an unspoken, visceral understanding coursed between them in which I had no part.

Years before, the father of a friend from college—a trim, angular tennis player of New England stock—stopped in on my parents when he was in Nashville for business. They had never met before. He was a direct person, artless yet charming. In her fashion, my mother welcomed him with a traditional southern breakfast—creamy grits, ham, sausage, eggs over easy, perfectly cooked. My friend's father had a bite here and there, commenting all the while on calories and cholesterol. When my mother recounted the morning to me, she sounded more bewildered than offended. Now she was bewildered again: her daughter had found a man who had the skills she had proudly determined not to pass on. "My daughter doesn't cook," she once bragged to a friend who was clearly confused by the boast. Now, here was her daughter, engaged to a man who did. "We marry our mothers," my friend Catherine once told me.

Their kitchen communion was probably the reason why my mother sat alone with John after that first meal, sharing intimate stories from her past. She talked about Mississippi and the joys and privations of her childhood. She talked about her parents: the pleasure her mother took in the natural world, and her father's military commitments that took the family to Germany for a year. She segued into stories about the racism she had experienced in the Jim Crow South. My mother was, like her mother, a true raconteur. In the telling of her stories, in all of their horrible richness, she showed John the scars of her anger and bitterness. I fought the urge to protest, to insist that he had nothing to do with her history, just as I, as a child, had not wanted to be claimed by the history of American racism. But I remained silent; the stories weren't for me. John was silent, too, ingesting her words as seriously and respectfully as he had consumed the food she served him. He knew she was explaining that her lovely home and exquisite meal were evidence of struggle and triumph, emblems of her resourcefulness and strength. When she cooked, she remembered and bested the past. In the kitchen, she created a new world. Her conversation was an invitation for John to enter and witness the miracle she had made.

My father had left the table, as usual, just after the meal. Eventually, I excused myself, too, leaving John holding a napkin-covered glass, tapping his fingers lightly on its sides, rocking his heels a bit to the rhythm of my mother's stories.

5.

"Emily's going to marry a preacher," snickered one of my Mississippi cousins to another as we lumbered along in my grandmother's car on a dirt road on a blazing August afternoon. I sat in the back by myself, my palms sticking to the buckling leather, my cheeks burning. I was twelve years old. I had been a bookish child who grew into a deeply self-conscious teenager. I appeared, I am sure, disconcertingly detached from the world around me. People sometimes found it hard to feel at ease in my presence. I may have been odd, but prim enough for a preacher I was not. No one saw the passion that burned inside.

I encountered people like me only as characters in books and on television. On the tube, I found my perfect white boy: Richard Thomas. He was loyal and prompt, arriving in our den every Thursday night to play the role of John-Boy on the television series *The Waltons*.

Like me, John-Boy was bookish, solitary, a dreamer. He was an intellectual, a poet. His artistic ambitions set him apart from everyone around him. His heart-shaped face, the large disc-like mole on his cheek, and his ever-present pout consumed me. He would understand me, I thought. Every week, I willed myself into the Walton residence where John-Boy and I would sit at their long wooden table and tell each other things we had never before said out loud.

John-Boy's turn on *Roots: The Next Generation* changed my life. It was the actor Richard Thomas, to be precise, who played Jim Warner on the sequel to the miniseries *Roots*. Like John-Boy, Jim was a lover of poetry. The only person who shared his love of art was a young black schoolteacher, Carrie Barden, who, like my parents, attended Fisk University. Carrie and Jim fell in love and eventually married. Their married life bored me; their secret courtship, however, I found thrilling.

For obvious reasons, no one could know that Carrie and Jim were becoming intimate. They developed delicious strategies to keep their secret, like discussing the work of Joel Chandler Harris while sitting back to back in Jim's carriage. Literature bound them. For Carrie, it was the source of her purity; for Jim, his passion. Carrie tried to resist, but she was pestered by dreams of Jim. On his part, nothing could keep Jim from Carrie, not the disapproval of his family, not even Carrie herself. "I will marry you!" he hollered as Carrie ran away.

I imagined that I should work on fashioning a disposition as modest and demure as Carrie's, but it just wasn't meant to be. Instead I recognized myself in Jim's furious passion, his fervor, recklessness, and the ferocious, boundless desire that lay just beneath the placid surface.

6.

Our trip to Hazlehurst was occasioned by a family reunion. About a month before the trip, John and I received a flyer in the mail describing the weekend events. We were living in Harrisburg, Pennsylvania, at the time. On the program was a list of all of the meals: a fish fry, country breakfast, and, finally, a barbecue on the family property that we call the Jefferson place, which consists of nearly two hundred acres, eighty-three of which are pristine woodland, save for a few acres cleared for family use. John started dreaming of the feasts long before we arrived in Nashville to join my parents for the drive to Mississippi.

The first event of the reunion, the fish fry on the Jefferson place, is already under way by the time we reach my grandmother's house. After introductions, John watches as my father sits down in the only easy chair in the room and becomes immediately engrossed in a baseball game. The women gather at the dining room table to trade details about a family squabble concerning reunion business that has soured feelings about the reunion altogether. Hours pass as the house buzzes with female muttering and the incessant droning of the television and air-conditioning unit. We miss the fish fry because the women are talking. We miss the fish fry because my father wants to watch baseball. No one asks John what he wants, not even me, caught up as I am in the savory details of the family feud. Eventually, my aunt Julia emerges with a plate of spaghetti covered with homemade sauce. She and John have enjoyed a warm relationship ever since.

Ever an optimist, John sets his sights on the country breakfast to be held the next morning, also on the Jefferson property. The family feud has not been resolved by the morning, however, and my father signals his intentions for the day by immediately descending into the overstuffed leather chair in front of the television. John tries to rally the family, but between the feud and my father we are stuck. He appeals to me, but I am riveted by the gossip and too intimidated, as always, by my father's silence to try to influence the course of the morning.

The final reunion event, a barbecue, is scheduled for the afternoon. John successfully herds my parents, aunt, and grandmother out the door. The heavy, heady smell of grilling meat saturates the air from a hundred yards away. We are spared the wilting sunshine by the awning of a gazebo that has been erected for the reunion. John peers excitedly around the brown bodies in front of him as my curious relatives, one by one, walk over to us and welcome him to the family.

We are near the front of the line when my father approaches, laughing and shaking hands all the way up to our place in line. He takes my elbow and says he wants to make it back in time for the second half of yet another baseball game. My father has ruled the family and we have always done as he pleased. There was never a choice. But now there is a choice. "We are not leaving until I get some of this barbecue," John says in a voice that is friendlier than the voice he used on the highway, but just as firm. I hold my breath, but my father goes back to glad-handing, ceding to John's assertion of authority just as easily as he had entrusted to him the steering wheel of his car. My mother, who has been watching, is clearly impressed—another story about John for her to tell.

John himself has told this story many times. I wince when he does because the family reunion story is a shameful reminder that, when presented early with an opportunity to perform the duties of a good wife-to-be, I failed. But that imaginary wife who wags her finger at me in judgment was not, and never had been, the kind of wife John wanted. At any rate, he has put up with my passive relationship with food as well as the more obnoxious elements of my personality. As for me, I endure regular critiques of the way I boil eggs. "We marry the problems," said another friend.

For my aunts, the family reunion story has served as a cautionary tale. They have made sure, in every subsequent visit, that the dining room table is crowded with food when John crosses the threshold. In fact, their favorite food story about John is set during one of those later visits. John entered the house, sweaty from the drive, and focused immediately on the mountain of food prepared in his honor. He dispensed quickly with greetings and headed toward the table, where he piled macaroni and cheese, collard greens, and potato salad onto a plate. Spiced, blackened shrimp and chicken wings coated in barbecue sauce disappeared into his mouth. That was the moment, my aunts say, when they knew for sure that, beyond and beneath his skin, John was one of them.

The gazebo that had been built for the reunion was the source of the family feud. My cousin George, my grandfather's nephew, lives in a trailer on the property. Some members of the family worried that after the reunion George would transform the structure into his personal workshop. They were right. Two years after the reunion, John and I sat beneath its shade among a collection of George's stuff: tools, car parts, a refrigerator, old washing machines, and fishing equipment.

Like most of the Jefferson men, George is solitary, reserved, and very tall. His dark-gray dreadlocks fall to his shoulders; his skin is a deep, even brown. He is a sometime carpenter, full-time jack-of-all-trades, a hunter of deer, and a collector of things. He is at ease in the natural world, so much so that it is hard to imagine him anywhere else, and even harder to imagine him in the New England in which John grew up. And yet the two men took to each other quickly. John teased him about the junk as the three of us sat under the gazebo. Both of them laughed when John nearly fell off a rickety lawn chair.

"Let's go fishing," George said to John. I stayed behind and stepped out from under the awning to enjoy the steady Mississippi heat and sunshine that my body craves during the long winters and cold, muddy springs in Vermont. They came back with a floppy freshwater trout that George gutted and fried on a grill, one of the only working pieces of machinery under the gazebo. The dirty chaos that surrounded us made it difficult for me to concentrate on the small glory of the meal. But John and George ate the flaky, delicate fish with their hands, sucking every morsel from its reedy bones.

When my mother and her sisters were young, the two man-made ponds on the Jefferson place were always stocked with fish, and the grounds were replete with family. Jeffersons lounged in rocking chairs on the wrap-around porch of the ranch-style home where my grandfather was born and raised. His brother and sister-in-law, called Brother and Sister, raised their thirteen children on the property. "It was like a fairground," my aunt remembers. Family and friends from all over Mississippi came on weekends to cook, eat, pick berries, and visit on the porch and grounds. The children played games and ate apples, peaches, figs, and plums from the trees that populated the land.

The Jefferson family inherited this Edenic place from its own Adam and Eve. The original owner of the property was Thomas James Jefferson and his wife, Susan (Susie) Keys Jefferson. Thomas James Jefferson was the son of a white man, a slave owner, whose surname was Meeks. Meeks had a common-law wife, possibly named Mary, who was black and a slave. The family story goes that Meeks essentially gave up the social privileges that went along with his white skin and lived with his black family for the rest of his life. His son, Thomas James, severed his ties to slavery by casting off the name Meeks when he became an adult and took on Jefferson instead. His brother, James Alfred, my great-great-grandfather, did the same.

Choosing a new name was not an uncommon practice among enslaved African Americans upon liberation. It may seem curious that Thomas James would renounce his ties to slavery by adopting the name of a slave owner, but his father would have grown up hearing a lot about President Thomas Jefferson, who died within a few years of Meeks's birth. Maybe he was intrigued by the relationship between Sally Hemings and President Jefferson, which had been a public scandal since the first term of Jefferson's presidency. Whatever the reason, Thomas James was hardly unique in his choice of surname. According to a recent Census Bureau survey, 75 percent of Americans with the last name of Jefferson are black. As a "black" name, it is surpassed only by Washington; 90 percent of people bearing that surname are African American.

My great-aunt was named Vergia Octavia Jefferson, but she was always called TJ, after her uncle, Thomas James. His father may have abandoned his whiteness, but at least some of his white descendants socialized with their black relatives; Aunt TJ would occasionally entertain them at her home. Her brother, my grandfather, however, like Malcolm X, despised the white blood that ran though his veins. He hated the fact that he was biologically bound to the Meeks family and wanted nothing to do with them. He counted some white people among his friends, but he didn't want them among his kin.

8.

John enjoys the Meeks-Jefferson story almost as much as I do. He and I talk a lot about race. We *like* racial difference—to experience it and then discuss it. There are interracial relationships in which each party claims not to see racial difference. I don't understand those couples and consider their relationships fundamentally humorless.

For John, race is a topic of intellectual interest and

aesthetic enjoyment. He listens to and writes about jazz, blues, and soul music. He has always had black friends, and I am not the only black woman with whom he has been romantically involved. "A white Negro," a friend smirked when I first described John to her. She meant it derisively, and I forgave her. I knew the barb was borne of envy. Her boyfriend was awkward. When he drove a car, he jerked his foot up and down on the brake, as if it were the pedal of a sewing machine. When John drives in the summer, he glides down the street with his elbow out of the window like a hero in a movie about noble neighborhood toughs. When we first met, I saw that he moved through the world with a fluidity that was both unselfconscious and theatrical. John would say that this is Italian masculinity, and that it has very much in common with black masculinity. One of the things first pointed out to me by the woman who introduced us, a black woman, was how well he could dance.

I was thirty-one when I met John. By that point, my father had taken a broader view on what kind of man I should choose for my husband. My father, who was born in Trinidad, liked the fact of John's Italianness right away. "Italians and Caribbeans," he said, "we care about food. We care about family." My father wasn't any more of a food person than I was in those days, and compared to my mother, at least, he spoke very little about his family. But he was clearly impressed by John, an intellectual who was unafraid of physical labor, who felt as content in front of a football game as he did inside of a book. He was something upon which my father and I could finally agree. I was surprised and annoyed by how much this pleased me.

"Emily needs someone to ground her," my father once said to my mother, who relayed his curious diagnosis to me. Because I had done all of the things they had expected of me—performed well in school and become a professor—I felt I had been grounded all of my life. The truth is that I have used my marriage to John as an opportunity to fly.

Our relationship was born at a way station. We met in New Haven at the home of a mutual friend. At the time John and I were living temporary lives in Harrisburg, Pennsylvania, and Cambridge, Massachusetts, respectively. When we decided to marry, I moved to Harrisburg to take an adjunct position at Penn State. We were in Harrisburg when we dreamed up a trip to Sapelo Island, one of the Sea Islands of Georgia located on the Atlantic coast of the southeastern United States. The culture and history of the place intrigued us as a site of resilient Africanness. For almost three hundred years, it has been home to the Gullah community of Hog Hammock. Sapelo is unique in that it is a state reserve whose livelihood, therefore, is not determined by the whims of tourists. This difference between Sapelo and its neighboring islands was obvious immediately after we landed. In the McIntosh County airport, black men from Jekyll and St. Simons stooped to heft the sleek leather suitcases and bulging golf bags of white men who ignored them.

It took two planes to get us from Harrisburg to McIntosh County, and both of them were delayed. It was after midnight when we arrived, and the ferry that took visitors to the island had shut down. An island resident offered us a ride on his motorboat. He, John, and I were alone on the still water that night. The moon looked heavy, worn, and marvelous. The water was the color of obsidian; it sparkled as it crested in gentle, thick waves. We got engaged the next day.

We met another interracial couple on the island, Sandra and Tim, a black woman and a white man, with a handsome big-eyed child. The five of us quickly became friends. Sandra and Tim laughed when I described the scene of the proposal. John was still on one knee, holding the box with the engagement ring, when a rattlesnake emerged from the woods and wriggled past us.

Sandra invited me for a walk. We sat on a bench near the water and she told me about the day her son was born. It was the middle of August, she said, and her skin had darkened. She was hot and huge, desperate to deliver. Moments after the birth, white nurses rushed inside her room, not to care for her but to see her baby's skin; they had made bets on what color it would be.

The food at our Sapelo hotel was unremarkable. If it weren't for John, I would not have registered this aspect of our stay, but an unwritten condition of our marriage has revealed itself to be that I improve my appreciation of the world of food. At first I faked it, then I became passably proficient, and finally I became sincerely interested. Over the years we have designed several vacations to suit our culinary curiosity. One summer, we used the guidebook *Road Food* as a compass. We began with an investigation into the country of barbecue: Memphis, New Orleans, and Texas. The quality of excellent beef was simple to appreciate, but the landscape of the Northwest stumped and overwhelmed me. My heart raced with terror as our drive into Wyoming took us into the clouds. I breathed deeply and read Willa Cather and Gretel Ehrlich in order to unlock the mysteries of the foreign world around me. We ate marbled, juicy steak on the same day as we visited the Badlands, whose rugged, ancient grandness made me nauseous.

9.

In its everyday incarnation, our marriage is generally mundane. We live with our two children in the suburbs in a house that resembles the house I grew up in. We are both professors who teach courses on African American culture. Unlike my television John, my real-life John was not exiled by his kin when he chose to marry a black woman. Unlike my white forefather Meeks, John has not felt compelled to renounce his whiteness, at least so far.

In *Their Eyes Were Watching God*, Janie Crawford has a revelation while marveling at a bee pollinating a bloom. "So this was a marriage!" She lay on her back and enjoyed the spectacle of a perfect union. For me, marriage is, in large part, the doing of laundry, tending of children and, of course, the preparing of food. The union between John and me is perhaps most fascinating when I see it through the eyes of other people.

"He refuses to pull the car up all the way into the driveway," I said to my friend Tanya once on the phone at the end of a long conversation about the routine domestic crimes our husbands had committed against us. "He says it's because of the icicles that form on the side of the roof. But it's July!"

"Marriage is hard," Tanya sighed, "but interracial marriage must be *really* hard."

I held the phone away from me and stared at the

receiver. Tanya is white, and so is her husband. I thought we had been talking as women married to men, that the grievances we held against our respective husbands had to do with sex and not race. Because it was not interracial anything that I had been complaining to her about, but rather the institution of marriage itself, which requires compromise, which is not always easy, at least for me.

"What's it like, being married to a white man?" asked Sophia at a college reunion as we walked together across campus. Sophia was born in Mexico. We hadn't seen each other in the twenty-five years since graduation. John and the girls were in town, too. He had just called to remind me that he didn't have the car keys. So, at that moment, being married to a white man was like being married to a man who needed the keys to the car in order to take our children to a museum. I knew she wanted emotional stories, dramatic stories, tales about struggle, uncertainty, and triumph. But the sun was shining, and I was taking a walk with someone whose company I had forgotten how much I enjoyed, so I only had funny stories to tell.

"Once, John said to me, 'When black people say, I haven't done such-and-such in a minute, they mean anything from an actual minute to several years,'" I said. We both laughed.

Then I told her the watermelon story. On the same trip to Hazlehurst that led us to George and his succulent trout, John and I stopped in town to buy a watermelon from a man selling them on the side of the road. The vendor was African American with salt-and-pepper hair; he wore a white T-shirt and jeans. I stayed behind in the air-conditioned car while John and the man chatted.

John, who was dressed in a light-blue T-shirt and worn, brown khaki shorts, put one hand on his hip and gestured with the other. I leaned back into the headrest and tilted the brim of my hat toward my eyes. John must be talking about one of his favorite summertime topics, I thought, which is how difficult it is to find a decent peach north of the Mason-Dixon line. When I peeked at them from beneath the brim, he and the man were still talking, bowing deeply as they laughed, like rocking toy penguins.

John balanced a watermelon in his hand as he returned to the car. I asked him what the man said to him and he smiled.

"He asked me how I was enjoying retirement," he said. We laughed a little together, and I remembered why I loved him, for not feeling diminished by being mistaken for some other white man, for not wanting to embarrass the man by pointing out his mistake, and for not taking an inordinate amount of pleasure in his error.

"What did you talk about for all of that time?" I asked.

John turned the car engine over and guided us back onto the road. "Fruit," he said.

This is what marriage to John is like, I told Sophia. I did not tell her about the period in our early courtship when, afraid of disapproving looks from strangers, particularly black strangers, I was reluctant to hold John's hand in public. I didn't tell her because I hardly think about that time anymore. And when I do, well, after fifteen years of laundry, child care, key retrievals, and egg-boiling debates, those days seem like episodes from another life.

10.

"Are you sure you want to do this?" my mother asked me a few months before the wedding. John and I were in Nashville taking care of last-minute plans. I sat on the edge of the bed in the dark room in which my mother spent most of her time in the last few years of her life. She turned on her side to face me. My mother's marriage had not been happy for a long time. She had endured many years of disappointment and isolation. Even though my father took good care of her as her health declined, the heft of all of those lonely years had worn her down.

"I think so," I said. I had planned the wedding she wanted for me, or so I thought. We were quiet. I waited for her to say more; perhaps she was waiting for the same. I had been waiting for a long time, storing up the joy I knew I would feel on the day she finally got up from her bed and smiled at the world again, maybe on the day of my wedding. But as I took her hand, my chest sagged with the understanding that I could not save her, not with a wedding, not with a son-in-law interesting enough to tell stories about, not with anything.

My mother passed away on a Christmas Eve morning. She was only seventy years old. It was early when I received a call from my brother informing me of her death. I sat on the edge of the bed, holding the phone, and touched John's arm.

"Mom died," I whispered.

In a single motion, John swung his body out of the bed and encircled me with his arm. On the way to the airport the highway was barren and dark—as dark as the night that held my grandmother as she fled from predatory white men, as dark as the stretch of the Atlantic Ocean that carried John and me to Sapelo. We held hands and drove in silence, both of us staring at the road ahead. This is marriage, I thought, or at least my marriage. It is not the stories of forbidden desire that thrilled me as a girl, or even magical rides through clouds and on dark waters. It is John's right hand in mine, and his left one sure and steady on the wheel.

Mother on Earth

Behold, children are a heritage from the Lord,
the fruit of the womb a reward.

—Psalms 127: 3–5

1. Selfish

I assumed I would conceive naturally when John and I decided to start a family. I didn't. We turned to fertility drugs with ambivalence. Reports of the mood swings the drugs sometimes caused worried me. I had only gotten through one round when I broke a wooden dish-drying rack over John's head. I don't remember what he said, but I'm sure it was something I would have otherwise considered innocuous. Instead a growling, uncontrollable rage emerged from nowhere and then overcame me like an emotional tsunami. We decided the drugs weren't for us.

Even if the drugs had taken, there would have been the aftermath of pregnancy to contend with. Having struggled with depression for as long as I can remember, I believed I would be a good candidate for postpartum depression. *That will be me,* I thought, whenever someone told me a story about a woman suffering from postpartum depression, so severe in one case that long-term care in a treatment facility was necessary. A mother of a teenager told me that she felt she had yet to return to her pre-pregnancy self. I wasn't sure that pregnancy would be worth it.

When I heard about couples that had invested tens of thousands of dollars in the struggle to conceive, I wondered if pregnancy would be worth it, literally. I wanted to spend my money on other things. I didn't say this out loud; it seemed like sacrilege. Sometimes I wondered if I was too selfish to get pregnant. Often I wondered if my infertility was some kind of holy judgment on my marriage or me. Always I wondered if other women wondered these things, or if there was something unnatural about my thoughts in particular. During all those months of wondering, I never once considered adoption, until I did.

I had gone along with fertility treatments for the same reason I went along other non-decisions I have made in my life, like having an enormous wedding: because people whom I loved wanted it for me. I thought I was *supposed* to want it, just like I was supposed to want to get pregnant by any means. Yet I cried genuine tears when, month after month, I was unable to conceive. I felt like a failure.

My friend Lisa, a scholar of the Bible, sat with me once as I confessed that another fertility treatment had failed to take. "This is your pain," she said. "You must bear witness."

Lisa was sitting across the room, but her words gripped me physically. I stopped crying. I was erect, alert, and full of purpose. From that moment, I paid attention to the more important presence in my insides: not the drugs but the little door in my heart that had always been closed to them. Behind that door was my truest self, and she didn't want to conceive that badly.

Not long ago, I read an interview with a famous actress

who adopted two children. When the subject of pregnancy came up, the actress said something like "It didn't interest me." It wasn't that pregnancy didn't interest me at all; it just didn't interest me *enough*.

Adoption, however, came naturally. One day I woke up and I knew. It hit me like a revelation. We were going to adopt, I told John, and then Lisa. We were going to adopt from Ethiopia. There is a notable Ethiopian-born population in Vermont, and a substantial number of them are adopted children. But to me the decision felt less practical than magical. I'm the kind of person who typically questions her instincts. In this case, I did not.

Sometimes people assume that my husband and I adopted for altruistic purposes. In truth, we adopted for the same reason that people pursue natural birth: because it was what we wanted. And for me, like any woman determined to conceive, like anyone who really wants anything, the question of money paled in comparison to my desire.

As it turns out, I *am* selfish. Adopting my daughters is the most self-centered thing I have ever done. It is the one decision I have made in my life that represents who I truly am, the only choice that aligns most squarely with my deepest and most fundamental belief about life on Earth: that we are here to see one another through this journey. We are here to keep our brothers. Our sisters, too.

Once we decided to adopt, signs seemed to spring up everywhere. I sat in a waiting room and opened a magazine to an article written by a woman who had adopted as a last resort and then conceived a second child naturally. Her greatest fear about adoption, she wrote, had been that she would not be able to bond with her child as intensely and authentically as a natural mother, that the bond between herself and her daughter would be, at best, only an approximation of that natural bond, or, at worst, simply counterfeit.

She discovered that they *were* different, her relationships with each of her two children, but the most fundamental difference between being the mother of an adopted child and being the mother of a biological child, she said, was that she was able to take public pleasure in the beauty of the child she had adopted. When strangers said of her adopted child, "What a beautiful baby!" she could respond without hesitation, "Yes, she is, isn't she?" But when strangers exclaimed over her biological child, she fumbled for a response. To agree, she explained, felt like vanity.

I hold her story in my heart.

2. Miracle

I was on the phone waiting for a picture I had forwarded to my friend Iris to open on her computer screen. I knew the picture intimately. It featured two brown babies with enormous eyes. One of them was in tears; the other one looked like she was trying not to laugh. Both of them were wearing crocheted yellow caps that made me think of Esther Williams.

Before we heard about the girls, John and I had never considered the possibility of twins. As the JPEG opened slowly on Iris's screen, she and I discussed this unexpected factor and all of the challenges it would present. When the

JPEG finally opened, Iris went quiet. Then she said, "Oh, you're fucked."

We were, indeed, happily fucked. There was no turning back. The question shifted from *How?* to *When?* What we assumed would be a straight line from us to the babies in the picture turned out to have close shaves and hair-raising detours. At one point, it looked like the adoption would fall through. John and I were in Ethiopia at the time. A government official told us to prepare ourselves for the worst. That night John and I held each other and sobbed. I was more terrified that night than I have ever been in my life; the anguish seemed to have no bottom to it. I thought of the babies in the picture, the perfect roundness of their eyes, the delicate curve of their feet, their dark, miniature hands. *They will have no memory of me,* I thought, *but I will remember them forever.* The next morning we soberly considered other options, like going for another round of drugs. Later I joked that I might be the only woman on Earth to pursue pregnancy because I couldn't adopt.

We hardly slept for the next seven days, keeping our phones close and checking our email almost hourly. Suddenly, the same official emailed to say that she had decided to approve the adoption. She didn't explain and we didn't ask why. I am still baffled and awed by the sudden turnaround that changed our lives forever. I routinely tell my daughters that they are my miracles, gifts from Providence itself, to which they respond with exasperation, "Mommy, *stop.*"

After a twenty-four-hour journey, we met John's mother, sister, and her two children at the airport in Boston. They burst into tears as the four of us deplaned. John drove us back to Burlington in the middle of a snowstorm. He was so exhausted that twice he pulled over to do jumping jacks in the snow in order to stay awake. He had no choice: when I took the wheel I nearly ran us off the highway.

The girls sat silent and staring in the back, looking like tiny Michelin Men in identical padded snowsuits. Eventually they fell asleep. When we finally arrived, and put them on our bed, they lay flat as boards. Suddenly, their eyes flew open. They looked at us and then peered around their fur-lined hoods and looked at each other. A feeling of peace seemed to settle between them. It lasted for a second. Then, as if on cue, they commenced to wail in unison until they passed out.

3. Counterfeit

During those dizzying early months, two good friends became pregnant in quick succession. I agreed to host their baby showers. No, I offered. Actually, I *insisted*. I consulted friends and the Internet for baby shower protocol, shopped for the right decorations, ordered cute cakes, all the while asking myself, *What are you trying to prove?*

At one of the showers, every single guest seemed to be pregnant, too. A woman I hardly knew put a newborn in my arms. Overwhelmed by feelings I didn't understand, I handed the baby back and went into another room to cry in private. What had my daughters looked like at that age? I tried to imagine their one-year-old faces pasted onto newborn bodies and cried some more. I would never know. I hated feeling so vulnerable, but even more than that, I hated that those feelings of vulnerability could be so easily triggered by a stranger. The fact that I had no control over those feelings frustrated me. I cried out of frustration, but also out of shame. I was ashamed of the secret envy I felt as I stood and chatted with women whose stomachs were as big as beach balls. I've heard adoptive mothers say that they wish they had originated their children. I know that if I had given birth to my daughters they would be wholly different people, and I like them just the way they are. Still, when I stand next to pregnant women, my stomach sometimes feels concave and hollow.

I no longer cry at baby showers, but the feeling of vulnerability, the experience of sudden exposure and, sometimes, the same shameful, secret envy of women who have successfully conceived compose a quiet, even current in my life as an adoptive mother. These feelings exist in the private chambers of my heart. In the very same chambers throbs the electric joy I experience as the mother of my daughters.

I never know how to respond when those negative feelings are triggered. Once a friend and I stood naked from the waist up as we changed clothes to go to an exercise class. "Look at those breasts that never nursed," she said wistfully. She meant it as a compliment. I was on the phone with the same woman a few weeks later and confided to her my worries about some problems one of my daughters was having in science class. "Well, they're not genetically yours, so at least you know it's not your fault," she said. Later, she explained that she had meant the comment to reassure me.

Both times I was caught completely by surprise, stunned by how quickly ordinary activities—changing clothes, an idle conversation with a friend—transformed into emotional landmines. I believe she meant no harm, but the effect of her comments was to remind me that I was not a biological mother. I don't need reminders. Even more disturbing was the fact that her comments revealed that she, herself, was constantly, even vigilantly, aware of the fact that I was not a biological mother. Her reminders touched my own quiet fear that my bond with my daughters might be missing something vital; that my maternity is an illusion and a lie.

I have found that another constant in my life as an adoptive mother is that other people often project onto me their essential feelings and beliefs about the mother-child bond. While we were in the process of adopting, one friend wondered aloud if true bonds were even possible between mothers and children who were not biologically related. This same friend confesses that there is little about her own daughter she finds familiar. Still, to her, to many people, the biological relation—blood—is supreme.

Several years ago, I told my daughters that I had made contact with their biological cousin.

"We already know all of our cousins," Isabella said.

"But this cousin is related to you by blood," I explained.

"'By blood,'" Giulia wondered. "What's that?"

Before I became a mother, I believed in the primacy of blood. Once I even said to one of my closest friends, who had decided to use a surrogate, that I was relieved she had chosen that route instead of adoption, because using a surrogate meant that her children would be "really" hers.

Today I am embarrassed and amazed, not only that I said those words, but even more that I actually believed them.

For me, adoption has been a journey from ignorance to enlightenment. What I understand now is that the difference between pregnancy and motherhood is something like the difference between having an enormous wedding and being married. But I'm not sure I would have found this out otherwise. In *Their Eyes Were Watching God* the main character shares with her best friend a few things she has found out about life over the years. "It's uh known fact, Phoeby, you got tuh *go* there tuh *know* there," she says. "Two things everybody's got tuh do fuh theyselves," she continues. "They got tuh go tuh God, and they got tuh find out about livin' fuh theyselves."

4. Romance

When I was a child I dreamed of being adopted, not only because the dynamics in my family sometimes mystified me, but also because the adoption stories I knew about sounded so romantic. I grew up in a community in which adoptions were kept hidden from children but whispered about among adults. Blood connections were revealed deliberately, at momentous junctures, like eighteenth birthdays, or recklessly, through overheard conversations. Adoption sounded to me like something out of a Charles Dickens novel, but in reality, these revelations created wounds that never healed. Happy families were perceived suddenly as fraudulent. Lives were thrown off track and personal histories reevaluated. *"No wonder he always . . ." "So that's why she never . . ."* That was forty years ago. Older relatives who are products of that era used to suggest that I keep the girls' identities as adoptees a secret from them. But they did not suggest what I should tell the girls instead. In order to keep such a secret, I would have needed an alternate narrative just as elaborate as the true story, considering the fact that my daughters' father is white.

Even though the adoption stories around me when I was growing up were shrouded in secrecy and pity, I knew of many people in the Deep South who raised children to whom they did not give birth. In fact, my grandmother was not ready to be a mother when my mother was born, so she entrusted my mother to her parents and siblings. My mother remembered her grandparents as upright, religious people who policed her posture and ate bacon with a knife and a fork. She adored them and described her years with her extended family as some of the happiest of her life. My mother called her grandmother "Mama" and her mother "Mother." To me, this said something about the different quality of intimacy she felt for each of her mothers. When I floated this theory by my mother, she considered it briefly, but she died before we got a chance to discuss it again.

When she was six, my daughter Isabella went through a phase during which she tried to figure out what to call me. For a while, she settled on stepmother. I felt tender amusement as I witnessed her trying to make sense of the nature of our relationship in her own mind. So far, it is only Isabella who has puzzled over what to call our bond. Not coincidentally, when I deny her something she wants, Isabella is the one to sometimes fling the barb that perhaps

BLACK IS THE BODY

all adoptive mothers fear: "You're not my *real* mother!" In one such instance I replied, "I am your mother on Earth. And you still can't wear your pajamas to school."

I am fascinated by the fact that my daughters never question the authenticity of their father's paternity, considering the racial difference between them. Isabella is happiest when she can begin and end her days with John. "Daddy, you should get a tattoo of me going like this," she told him years ago, mugging like Shirley Temple. At around the same time, she informed me calmly that it would be most convenient if I died first, so that her daddy could take care of her without my interference. John is the one she goes to when she has a bad dream. "You can't comfort me the way Daddy does," she once explained to me gently. Even when John becomes irritated by the chaos that the girls create and leaves the room, Isabella trails behind him, an identical scowl on her face and a stuffed animal under her arm.

"No one on Earth wants to be with me as much as Isabella wants to be with you," I sometimes complain to John. He pats my shoulder pityingly, like a prince dispensing coins to a pauper.

5. Holy

My daughters' biological mother is dead, but she is an active presence in our lives. Isabella says her birth mother appears in her dreams and sometimes signals her presence by turning the light on and off in their room. "She is your mother in heaven," I tell her, "and she entrusted you to me." Like a divine priestess, like a holy ghost, I believe she blesses our union.

"Adoption is a holy sacrament," said the priest at a ceremony my parents arranged to welcome our daughters into our church family in Nashville. I believe this is true. I have the same feelings about adoption as I do about zebras, in whose astonishing, majestic presence I think, *This must be God at work.*

When we met the girls' maternal grandmother, she said I was her daughter returned to her from the dead. She compared me to Mary, Mother of God. I was glad; I felt unworthy. I felt her quiet agony over her daughter's death. I looked at my new daughters and realized immediately that I would spend my life trying to reconcile myself to the terrible coincidence that brought about our union, and the fact that my greatest joy was occasioned by someone else's tragedy.

But tragedies happen. People die and the living must take up where the dead left off. This is our duty; this is our joy. A friend once told me that she had never felt more like a woman than when she was pregnant. When the girls were placed in my arms, I had never felt more deeply human.

6. Bounty

Our daughters have known they were adopted from the moment they were capable of knowing anything. Some stories about adoption emphasize poverty or lack; a child unwanted or abandoned, a lost history. The stories we tell the girls are about bounty. You are adored on two continents, I tell them. You have two worlds, two countries, two languages, and two stories to tell about how you came to be. So far, this strategy seems to be working. One of their favorite babysitters did not know they were adopted until the girls told her. The babysitter reported to me that in response to this news she had said, "Ohhhh," in a high pitch and put on a sympathetic face. Giulia knew the look. "Well, it's not *sad*," she explained.

For as many Ethiopians as there are in Vermont, exponentially more live in Washington, D.C. When the girls were two years old, we traveled to D.C. to meet our Ethiopian adoption liaison for dinner. It was his first visit to the United States. He had spent the day playing tourist, visiting monuments and museums. "Americans," he said, "you know how to preserve your stories."

We all met up at Queen of Sheba, one of the many Ethiopian restaurants in Washington. When I took Isabella to the bathroom, Giulia agreed to stay behind with the waitress, a beautiful young woman in traditional dress, who knelt and held Giulia's hands.

"Twins?" asked the waitress when Isabella and I emerged from the bathroom. I nodded.

She asked me what part of Ethiopia they were from.

"Tigray," I said.

I knelt with Isabella while the waitress began to speak to Giulia in Tigrinya. Giulia alternately nodded and shook her head.

Then, Giulia looked at me and put her arm around my neck. She pulled me closer as her conversation with the waitress seemed to pull her deeper and deeper into memory. *You belong to me,* said her fierce two-year-old grip. I leaned in until our bodies made a bridge between the present and the past. With all of my might, I assured her through my skin, *And you belong to me.*

We do belong to each other. But Giulia and Isabella also belong to something and somewhere else. They belong to a history preserved in the recesses of their minds and hearts; in their bodies, too, perhaps down to the level of the cell. Where the girls' identities reside in the worlds between past and present, there and here—that is a story they will make up on their own.

There is one story that is unequivocally true, and that true story goes like this: I am their mother on Earth, their here and now. The one who prepares them for spelling quizzes, smells their breath to make sure they've brushed their teeth, and nags them to tidy their room—that's me. I am the present and, with any luck, the future, too. As they grow older, questions about their past will not be the only ones I won't be able to answer. They will come upon other mysteries in their lives, and I will encourage them to view the mysteries of life as vitalizing and not crippling. But like everyone else who resides on Earth, they will have to go there to know there and, ultimately, find out about living for themselves.

Black Is the Body

Black History

My brown daughters became black when they were six years old. They were watching television one day in February, Black History Month. A commercial came on. It was more like a thirty-second history lesson, a commemoration of a pilot, a poet, or a politician; a First Black, as a writer I know calls them. *Them* being the racial pioneers, the inaugural Negroes, the foremost African Americans to break through racial barriers in their chosen fields. By "break through," I mean, of course, secure the regard of white people.

"See, we're black," Giulia said to Isabella.

"No, we're brown," Isabella responded.

"Yeah, but they call it black," Giulia explained.

Despite my efforts to shield them, my daughters had somehow gotten wise to the absurd and illogical nature of American racial identity. Blackness, Giulia had figured out, had nothing to do with actual skin color. Blackness, she had come to understand, was an external identity, external to her, anyway. Race was something other people identified, something they *said* but not necessarily *saw*. Blackness, she had intuited, was a social category; not a color but a condition. And like it or not, it was time, she was informing her sister, to get with the proverbial pro-gram. In spite of me, but also because of me, my brown daughters were becoming black.

My heart sank.

It was not blackness per se that caused my heart to sink. I enjoy being black. But it took me a long time to get here, to this place of racial pleasure. My earliest expe-riences of blackness were defined by an unpleasant and uncomfortable hypervigilance. Being black meant that you had to be constantly aware, that you could never really be at ease. Early on, I got wise to the fact that being black in a white place meant that the world was not a safe place, not for you.

In my family, race was not a construction, or a theory, or an outdated consequence of history, but the active, liv-ing foundation of our reality. Race determined the con-tours of every choice we made; every mundane public act we performed was a project with a name. When we moved into our house, it was called *integration*. When my older brother and I entered the public school system, it was called *desegregation*. The split between black and white was not metaphorical; railroad tracks divided black and white Nashville. On the white side of town, South Nashville, we played a role in a grand project of enormous proportions. We lived in South Nashville, but in North Nashville we could be black in a way that was not possible in any other part of the city. In North Nashville, no one white was watching. We could relax. We were free.

North Nashville was where my father practiced medi-cine and where we attended events at Fisk University, my parents' alma mater, and one of this country's oldest historically black colleges and universities, or HBCUs. North Nashville was where we attended church in a small chapel that was established for the faculty and students of Meharry Medical College, from which both of my parents received their graduate degrees. Among the parishioners in the chapel were men and women I called Aunt and Uncle even though we had no biological relationship. We shared something bigger and more profound than blood: history. Inside the church we celebrated our belief in God and a common pride in how we all made it over and broke through. We were a community, a black community, built in spite and because of racism. Because if it had not been for white supremacy, schools like Fisk and Meharry might never have existed.

But my daughters were not born under the shadow of this history. They are black by ideology and affinity, but not by blood. When they were twelve months old, they assumed dual citizenship in both America and African America.

Once, when we were out of town visiting John's extended family, I told them the Black History Month story. I could see that the story unsettled them. I tried to explain my reasons for having wanted to protect my daughters from the language of race, but my explanations seemed only to make them more impatient. "Don't you want them to know their history?" John's cousin asked.

I knew what she meant. She meant American slavery, segregation, and the civil rights movement; Frederick Douglass, Sojourner Truth, and Rosa Parks; Martin, Malcolm, and other First Blacks. February stories, which, as American stories, belong to her, this white American woman, more than they do to my daughters.

"I am an African who lives in America," Isabella explained one day. She was recounting a conversation she had had with a third-grade classmate. The African Children's Choir had come to Burlington, and the class had taken a field trip to see them perform. Later that day, Isabella's classmate, in an attempt to identify the difference she perceived between Isabella and the children on stage, had referred to Isabella as an African American. Isabella corrected her: "While the law may state that I am an American, I am African."

"When I came to this country . . ." she continued. Astonishment made it difficult for me to continue paying attention. That my daughter had such a fine sense of her place in the world I had not known. Her implicit assessment of my role as essentially a porter in this stage of her life journey felt wholly appropriate.

My daughters and I flip through picture books of twelfth-century Ethiopian underground churches carved out of rock. I show them websites that feature both centuries-old drawings and modern photographs of Ethiopian kings and queens. "Yours is the only African country to fight off the colonizer," I remind them often. Every mother thinks her daughters look like angels, but my daughters *do* resemble the doe-eyed, haloed brown cherubs that dominate Ethiopian Orthodox Christian iconography.

"Why did white people make black people slaves?" Isabella asked one February afternoon.

"There's been slavery all over the world," I told her. "Even in Ethiopia."

I am proud that my daughters were born in a world

where not only slaves but also angels and aristocrats look like them.

In the world in which I grew up, Jesus was blond and blue-eyed. I almost got into a fight in high school when I informed a white classmate that Jesus probably had brown skin and definitely had hair like lambs' wool. My classmate was just as baffled as he was enraged. He was as blond and blue-eyed as, well, Jesus—or Santa Claus, upon whose whiteness television show host Megyn Kelly once insisted. Having grown up in a culture whose icons looked like him, how could information like the news I shared about Jesus not shake my classmate to the core?

I envy my daughters' history, as have African Americans since the time when we were Negroes.

"To know where the Negro is going one must know where the Negro comes from," writes Trinidadian writer and activist C. L. R. James in his 1939 essay "The Destiny of the Negro." He castigates capitalist pseudoscientists for attempting to "deprive the Negro of any share in the famous civilizations of Egypt and Ethiopia." Before him, W. E. B. Du Bois—author, activist, social scientist, statesman, and arguably the preeminent First Black in American history—composed *The Star of Ethiopia,* an American historical pageant, which opened in New York in 1913. The play, which, in one of its productions used almost one thousand actors, attempts to capture black history in its entirety.

Du Bois described the drama in his essay "The Star of Ethiopia: A Pageant": "It begins with the prehistoric black men who gave to the world the gift of welding iron," he wrote. "Ethiopia, Mother of Men, then leads the mystic procession of historic events past the glory of ancient Egypt, the splendid kingdoms of the Sudan and Zymbabwe down to the tragedy of the American slave trade. Up from slavery slowly . . . the black race writhes back to life and hope . . . on which the Star of Ethiopia gleams forever."

My daughters' connection to Africa does not have to be fashioned or dramatized, invented or recuperated. It is a concrete reality to which many African Americans aspire; that aspiration is represented in the term "African American" itself. So much of the complexity of being African American inheres in the fact that we are, in fact, Americans, products of this soil yet rooted in something, somewhere else.

Becoming American

"One ever feels his two-ness,—an American, a Negro; two souls, two thoughts, two unreconciled strivings; two warring ideals in one dark body, whose dogged strength alone keeps it from being torn asunder," writes Du Bois in his 1903 classic, *The Souls of Black Folk*.

When I was growing up, some of my West Indian cousins found the unreconciled strivings of African Americans tiresome and confusing. Educated in the States at HBCUs, they exasperated their classmates by insisting that black alienation was self-imposed. Why couldn't black people embrace a national identity? asked my cousin Anita. She claimed she couldn't understand it. I was not surprised when she returned to Trinidad after college.

During a trip I made to the island with my family as a teenager, a couple of years after Anita left the States, I tried to get her to identify one of her friends in the clumsy, ill-fitting American racial terminology that she had come to detest (it was, after all, the only terminology I had to use).

"Is he biracial?" I asked her about a young man to whom she had introduced me. "Indian and Chinese? Black and white?"

"He's Trinidadian," she said, managing, somehow, not to roll her eyes. The conversation ended as abruptly as did her relationship to America. What had been promoted by her elders, including my father, as a land of professional opportunity, proved to her to be an intolerable ideological straitjacket.

My father was different. Unlike some of his nieces and nephews, he embraced blackness, threw himself into it with a kind of romantic fervor. He landed on these shores from Trinidad at the dawn of the civil rights movement, and his passion for blackness intensified with the rise of the Black Power movement. "Black," he remembers, was a term coined by Black Power activist Stokely Carmichael, who was my father's contemporary in age and a fellow Trinidadian.

"When did you become black?" I asked my father as I began to write this essay. As he reminisced, I considered the parallels between him and Carmichael: both graduates of HBCUs (Carmichael went to Howard), both christened with undeniably British names (my father's first and middle names are Harold Oswald), and both, as children, subjects of the Crown.

My father took to blackness quickly, but Americanness—

not so much. I remember joking around once at the dinner table with my brothers as my father stared at us as if we were from outer space. "Where did I get these American children?" he wondered out loud.

For my father, blackness was in *here*, organic and natural, but Americanness was *out there*, a consequence of chance and opportunity. He might have wound up in England if it hadn't been for his uncle, another graduate of Meharry, who offered him America, where he begot children who would not only grow up on the other side of what appeared to him—at least that night at the dinner table—as an unbridgeable, ineffable divide, but who would also continuously frustrate him by mispronouncing words like "ad*ver*tisement."

Valentine

February has proven to be a weighty month for the brown girls in my house.

In her final year of preschool, Isabella found herself in the middle of a romance. Ever since she was a toddler I have felt prescient pity for the boys who will fall in love with Isabella. Once they have fallen, I am certain they will not be able to find their way back out. Gilbert was the name of the first boy who tumbled. He was an affable child, tan and green-eyed, with long, dark eyelashes and round, dimpled cheeks. Exceptionally tall for his age, Gilbert always seemed to be standing around with his hands in his pockets whenever I came to retrieve the girls. However, there was one time I saw him stand behind Isabella, who was busy at a craft table, and unaware of Gilbert as he gathered her braids lightly and let them fall, over and over, gather and fall, his eyes full of wonder, as if he were playing with a magical beaded curtain.

In October, Gilbert invited Isabella to his birthday party. The girls and I had a conflicting engagement, so Isabella told him she would be unable to attend. Gilbert's mother called; her son was beside himself, she said. He admired Isabella, in part because she had never been sentenced to a stint in the "blue chair," the punishment chair, where he himself spent a fair amount of time. Her smile made him happy, he told his mother. In lieu of the birthday party, she asked if Isabella could come over the next afternoon for a playdate. Even though it was a weekday, I was moved by Gilbert's plight, so I agreed. I thought Isabella would at least be amused when I informed her of the degree of Gilbert's fondness, but she only shrugged.

When I went to pick up Isabella, Gilbert's mother and I chatted while our children said good-bye. Isabella gave Gilbert one of her signature bear hugs. His arms dropped to his sides and a stunned, glassy look spread over his face. It was the look of love, pure and true.

After the playdate, Gilbert stepped up his game. He asked Isabella on an actual date. ("What did you say?" I asked. "Well, I told him I couldn't cut *school*," she told me.) And then, in early February, he told her he was going to draw a Valentine's Day card with a picture of them kissing on the lips. He wrote her a note I found in her backpack. "Your hair is pretty," read his four-year-old scrawl. He signed it with a drawing of a heart.

But a week before Valentine's Day, Gilbert told Isabella that he was only going to give the light people cards that year. She would get her card the following year, he promised.

I didn't hear about this until bedtime, when so many revelations come to light. My first—and last—instinct was that Gilbert had not meant the comment maliciously. But Isabella told me that what he said had hurt her feelings. I emailed their teacher. It was important, I believed, that she know that race—racial difference—had reared its head in her classroom in a potentially destructive way.

The next day, the teacher arranged a sit-down between the kids. Gilbert offered an apology, which Isabella accepted and—according to Isabella and the teacher—the two of them spent the rest of the day playing happily together.

What changed in Gilbert? I may never know. Surely, someone, something, got to him and made him look at Isabella differently. In general, Gilbert was aware of Isabella in a way that she was not aware of him. She was used to seeing white people; he was not used to seeing brown people. I believe he was trying to make sense of what it meant for him to care for a girl whose skin was so different from his. Years from now, he will be embarrassed at having said such a thing, or at least that's what I like to imagine.

That's what happened to my friend's grandfather, an immigrant from the Netherlands. One of the first people he met when he arrived in the States was a black man. They shook hands, and my friend's grandfather looked down at his palm, expecting the black man's brownness to have rubbed off on his own hand. The best part of the story, my friend told me, was that whenever his grandfather repeated this anecdote, he always said, "Somewhere, right now, there is a black man telling a story to his family about that fresh-off-the-boat Dutch guy who thought the color of his skin was some kind of hoax."

Every time I am reminded of this story, I think of the exchange that took place between Malcolm X and Alex Haley in a U.S. airport. Haley was admiring an arriving family of European immigrants. They were about to learn their first word of English, Malcolm predicted: "nigger."

A Regrettable Choice

I have heard it said that a rite of passage in every black parent's life is the moment when his or her child comes home and asks, "What does 'nigger' mean?"

I don't remember bringing the question to my parents, but I'm sure I must have, because I cannot remember a time in my childhood when I did not know what it meant. For as long as I can remember, I knew that "nigger" meant to be different, to be outside, to be less.

The first time my daughters heard the "n-word," as it's often called, I was the one who said it. I had given a talk on my work on the white author and archivist Carl Van Vechten and his personal and professional involvement in the Harlem Renaissance at a book festival in Woodstock, Vermont. My daughters wanted to come, and I consented on the condition that they sit quietly and pay attention. Not five minutes into my talk, they had made their way up to the podium and begun tussling over the pointer.

Later, I accused Isabella of going back on our agreement and not paying attention. "I was paying *play*tention," she explained, "playing and paying attention."

"Okay, then what was my talk about?" I asked her.

"It was about a white man who made a regrettable choice in the title of his book."

"Do you remember the title?"

"No. What was it?"

"Forget it. It has a bad word in it," I said.

"Was it the F word? The H word? The S word?"

No, no, and no.

I was able to distract her from the topic until later that evening, when she introduced the mystery to Giulia, who ran down the same list of consonants. Finally, I relented. The title was *Nigger Heaven*, I said. The word was "nigger." What does it mean, they wanted to know? I hesitated. It was a big moment, a moment I had been dreading since before I became a parent, and I was not prepared. "It's a bad word white people sometimes use to put black people down," I finally told them. *Well, that's it*, I thought. *Their childhood is over.* They were quiet for a moment. Then, Giulia put her hand on her hip. "Well, that's rude," she said. I reared back. It *is* rude, I thought, and maybe that's all it will be for them.

About a week later, Giulia came home from spending time with a neighborhood girl—eleven years old and white—who told her and her sister that a person could get arrested for using the "m-word," Giulia reported.

"It's the n-word," I said. "It's the word we talked about a while ago."

"No, it's the *m-word*. Two lumps," Giulia corrected me, and held up two fingers in a peace sign.

B Words

Donna is the name of the neighborhood girl. In the summer, she drops her bike in the front yard and thunders through our house in her dirty bare feet, on the hunt for my daughters. She runs up to the girls' room where they each insist that she piggyback them around the house. Then, the three of them tromp up and down the streets of our neighborhood, hopping from pool to pool, outfitted in slick, wet bathing suits and mismatched flip-flops, with tight towels girdling their hips. I watch them from my window. This is what childhood should look like, I think. Outside of this frame, racial discord grows and persists. But inside of the frame is a world that I could never have imagined when I was growing up.

But the South of my childhood has changed, too. Shortly after the historic 2008 presidential election, I took a trip to Nashville and saw a bumper sticker on the back of a pickup truck that read, "Rednecks for Obama: Workin' for the man who'll do more for the workin' man." There was a good ole boy at the wheel and a gun rack in the back. From that moment, my story about Nashville had a new chapter.

My daughters will have their own stories, and the ones I tell in these pages may or may not describe them, or even interest them at all. In fact, while watching television with Giulia on another February day, I asked her if she remembered the exchange she had with her sister while they were watching television during Black History Month two years earlier. She didn't.

"You know, the thing you said about being black," I prodded.

"I'm not black," Giulia said. "I'm brown like you."

"I'm brown *and* black," I told her, realizing this truth for the first time.

It is in here and out there, my racial identity; it is something I have both lived and learned. My racial sense of self is made of rage and faith, pain and joy; it's a sensory cocktail I remember experiencing every time I heard my church aunts and uncles tell the tales—black tales—about how they made it over and broke through. By black I mean *black,* not African American; I was born in the same era in which my father was reborn, in the wake of civil rights and the first stirrings of Black Power, and all of their attendant pageants of glorious struggle and triumph. It goes deep, beyond the skin, the organic racial romance that informs everything I do, and everything I write. I am black—and brown, too: Brown is the body I was born into. Black is the body of the stories I tell.

Skin

Thomas and his six-year-old daughter Meghan come over for a visit. Our living room is a tight space, so our bodies touch when Meghan and I sit side by side on the couch. For a while, we listen to the conversation between Thomas and John. Meghan touches my hand tentatively, and I understand that she wants to examine the thick silver band I wear on my middle finger. She turns my hand over to study the ring from another angle. I admire her profile, which is nearly obscured by her stick-straight blond hair. She leans forward, turns her own hand over, and puts our exposed palms side by side.

The dark etchings on my palm have never looked as bold, as thick, as mysterious, as they do now, set against hers, which are nearly invisible, more impressions than actual lines. Married to a white man, having had white friends all of my life, I must have noticed this difference before, but I don't remember the initial experience of discovery.

Meghan and I are mesmerized. We hold our palms perfectly still while the room goes quiet. Meghan's father gently pulls her hand away from mine. He smiles at me. His eyes seem to offer an apology. The men resume their talk.

Out of the corner of my eye, I see that Meghan is looking down, her hands folded in her lap. My face is hot and I shift in my seat, uncomfortably aware of the nearness of our bodies. The current of mutual curiosity that had united us has been smothered under a heavy blanket of shame.

Thomas doesn't want me to feel like an object of study, for Meghan to examine me as she did my ring. He wants to save his daughter, too, from being an unwitting perpetrator of a kind of exoticization. One of the reasons I like Thomas is because he is the kind of white person who is sensitive to these things, attentive to what it must feel like to be black in a white place. But just as much, I think, he simply does not want Meghan to see the difference between us. The problem is, she does.

I had not felt studied or exoticized by Meghan. I had not felt like a curio or an artifact. I had felt like a woman with beautiful hands. I felt only tenderness for the child and her wonder at my palm. The pleasure she took in our difference pleased me.

A few years later I became a mother.

"Mommy, what color is Daddy's skin?" asked Giulia. She was three years old. I had just packed her and her sister into the car to take them to preschool. Through the open window they waved good-bye to John before he turned and went back into the house.

I panicked. Just a few days before, my friend Tina told me that her son had recently made a reference to a "black guy" at school. She panicked. It turned out her son meant a guy wearing a black shirt.

"Do you mean what color is Daddy's shirt?" I asked.

"No," Giulia responded. "I mean what color is Daddy's *skin*."

"It's tan," I began carefully. "Daddy's family is from Italy. Your skin is brown because you were born in Ethiopia. Mine is brown because my family is from the United States and Trinidad."

She was silent. I was relieved.

At that point, the four of us were leading Crayola lives. Except for the hours my daughters were in preschool, we lived in the bubble of the four of us, a family, the skin of whose members ranged from Almond to Sepia, according to the Crayola Color Chart. Before they came to know race, I wanted them to enjoy color. In my mind, in my experience, they were distinct: race was trauma; color was beauty. Between race and color was the distance between our public and private lives. I maintained the distance for as long as I could. I resented it when the distance collapsed. My resentment had less to do with the introduction of the language of race into our vocabulary, and more to do with my inability as a mother to enable my children to define the world on their own terms. I wanted their world to be different from the one I had inherited. The language of color sounded like the freedom I craved, freedom from my own past—for them and for me.

I can't help it, or so it appears. I carry the trove of my mother's stories inside of me, like an organ. I adorn myself with them, like jewels or thorns on a crown. Stories of her rage, pain, and bewilderment over what she had witnessed and experienced as a black girl growing up in the Jim Crow South. Because she was a skilled narrator, I felt my mother's stories as much as heard them. Now I tell them myself, because they are interesting, because I can't resist stories that can be felt as well as heard, and because I feel a need, both obligation and urge, to keep them alive. My mother felt the same need; the stories did not belong to her exclusively. Some of them she had inherited from her mother and grandmother just as plainly as she had inherited from them the shape of her legs and the moles on her neck. My mother's family had no money. Their name was inherited from a white man. Am I maintaining our only legacy, or am I perpetuating the pain of the past? Is the telling the salve or the wound?

"It's strange to me," I say to Shanté, a friend and former student who is visiting from New York. "The girls don't approach white people with the same wariness, even fear, that I do."

"That's because they're growing up in a house with a white person who loves them," Shanté replies.

As my daughters become more interested in the world and my past, I tell them my mother's stories, which they find curious but alien. Indeed my mother's stories describe a world that seems light-years apart from the one in which they were born, and the one in which they live now.

One day when she was in the third grade, Isabella told me she had a story about something that happened to Giulia that day on the bus ride home from school.

"Don't tell her," Giulia whispered to her sister, and I knew the story was about race. She knew I would leap to her defense, or overreact, which my daughters tell me that I do so much that overreacting is just the way I react. Giulia did not want me to react or defend her. In other words, she did not want me to claim the story as my own.

Isabella told me anyway. Another third grader, a boy called Farhan, announced to the other kids on the bus that he would "never marry a girl with skin as dark as Giulia's," Isabella said.

I tried to keep the heartbreak out of my eyes as I turned to Giulia, who was petting Shadow, her stuffed cat. "I didn't care," she said.

"You did!" insisted Isabella. "You should have seen your face."

What happened after the insult was more remarkable to me than the slight. Patrick, a classmate and friend who lives nearby, a white boy, stood up and denounced the comment as racist. Other kids followed suit.

"The same kind of thing happened to me when I was growing up," I told my daughters. "But no white kids ever stood up for me."

Upon first hearing it, I feared the incident had hurt Giulia. But the insult is not the part of the story that Giulia carries. In fact, she prompts me to tell it now, when adult friends come over.

"How did you feel?" Estelle asked Giulia when she heard the story.

"I could have beaten him up," Giulia said, "but I didn't."

In her evolving life narrative, the bus story is about herself as a source of power, not as an object of humiliation.

"I know that when the girls go out with John, they're going to come back," I say to Shanté, who nods. She knows I am talking about the killings of black men and women that now seem routine, the parade of deaths that feed the news at a steady march. I mean that the girls are going to come back alive, and that this is because of the color of John's skin.

If I have done nothing else in this life, I have given my children a father who loves and protects them. My daughters enjoy the shelter of his strong, solid, male body, which they use as furniture: stool, armchair, and bed. They don't know it now, but the color of his body, his skin, is also a shelter, a shield, but only as long as they stay close.

When she was four years old, I teased Isabella once about who she might marry. "Your mother would be very disappointed in you," she responded gravely. For starting such a conversation with a four-year-old girl, she meant, or maybe starting such a conversation with anyone at all.

Then she said, "I'm going to marry a man. A man with skin a different color than mine."

"I—" I started, having no idea what to say next.

She cut me off. "It's my choice."

Much later, she explained that she meant someone who looked like her father. And why shouldn't she be free to choose someone like John? She has made a home of his body. Of course she would imagine a faraway future with a man whose skin is the same color and texture as that of the current love of her life.

At a summertime gathering of friends, a black woman who is married to a white man describes a situation at work. A white colleague complimented her on the light color of her children's skin. Not wanting to jeopardize the work relationship, not wanting to be cast as "oversensitive," my friend accepted the compliment.

"I wondered what Paul would say," she says. Paul is her husband.

Before she can finish her sentence, before she can get past *what*, another black woman with a white husband interrupts. "What a *free* person would say?" she offers.

The black women in the group, including me, laugh hard, brittle laughs, the kind of laughs that recognize painful truths. Our white friends and husbands remain silent.

The black woman with a white husband who equates whiteness with freedom is me.

Much later, I realized what I wanted to say to Isabella. I wanted to warn her about the dangers of being a black woman, the vulnerability of our bodies. I heard my father's voice, *White boys are only after one thing,* and felt my throat fill with disgust, less for him than for myself.

. . .

At a bed-and-breakfast in Hampton, Virginia, I become friendly with Barbara, the proprietor, a black woman, and a native Virginian. She gives me visitors' guides and advice on tourist attractions until I finally confess that I have come almost solely to be among black people, to see dark skin, and for this pleasure, I don't need to see anything or go anywhere but up and down the city streets. She nods, accepts my confession, but cannot fully empathize. She lives and works among black people, so how could she?

Before I arrived, I had imagined I would keep to myself during my visit to Hampton, which I had planned as a brief respite from my roles as wife and mother. Instead I spend my time telling stories about my family to whoever will listen. Barbara is a good listener. After breakfast, she sits down with me at the table while I linger over coffee. She is still in her apron, her body turned toward me, one arm on the table, the other draped over her chair, her whole self a sign of reception.

I tell her what I said to Shanté.

"White parents teach their children how to live," she says. "We have to teach our children how to survive."

My daughters are laughing and playing at the Farmer's Market in Burlington. A game of tag commences. They choose me as a base, ducking back and forth behind and in front of me. Behind me, Isabella puts her hands on my hips to steady herself as she dodges Giulia's touch. I cover Isabella's hands with mine. I want to say something. *Don't act so . . .* What is it that I want to say? *Don't act so . . . free.*

I don't say them, but the words sound in my head as clear and loud as a chime.

"You are not a little white girl," my mother sometimes said to me when I was young and willful. I resented her words; I knew they were meant to hold me in place, somehow, and force my eyes open to the world as it was. I didn't understand at the time that she was trying to protect me, as well.

In Hampton I walk the city streets, arms swinging, chin up toward the May sun. Not only have I come to see brown people, I have also come to escape the gray days of nascent spring in Vermont. In the eyes of passersby I might be a woman, a black woman, or a person who appears to be taking a peculiar amount of pleasure in the sunshine. No matter what, here in Hampton, I am not alone.

Years ago I sat on a panel in the Burlington public library with other Vermonters, white and black. The panel had been organized as part of a community discussion about an incident that occurred in 2009 in Cambridge, Massachusetts. Henry Louis Gates Jr., who is African American and a scholar of international prominence, was arrested upon breaking into his own home after discovering his front door was jammed. Discussion veered from the incident itself to the state of race relations in Vermont. Black participants spoke about the challenges of living black in this state. In the course of the discussion, the South Burlington chief of police, another panelist, had occasion to say, "Dark skin stands out in a white place."

He offered the comment flatly but kindly. Like Shanté's insight, I experienced it as simple truth.

If only sight itself were that simple. Because the problem is not the visibility of dark skin, but who sees it and what the viewer feels motivated to do next.

People see it but are afraid to say so. It is dangerous to talk about racial difference these days. You might, God forbid, be called a racist, which is, in the eyes of some people, akin to being declared a murderer. So we resort to the seemingly safe terrain of color-blindness, which can be a kind of violence, an aggressive act of willful ignorance.

"I am invisible, understand, simply because people refuse to see me," explains the narrator of *Invisible Man*. "Like the bodiless heads you see sometimes in circus sideshows, it is as though I have been surrounded by mirrors of hard, distorting glass. When they approach me they see only my surroundings, themselves, or figments of their imagination—indeed, everything and nothing but me."

"I thought we weren't supposed to see race anymore," whispers my student Dusty at the end of class one day. The course is Race and the Literature of the American South. It counts as a "diversity course"; students at the University of Vermont are required to take a certain number of them. These courses are meant to serve as doses of intellectual tonic whose aim is to introduce sheltered students to experiences of people that do not look like them. They are crash courses in and against bigotry; twelve weeks on the intellectual antibiotic and you are, presumably, cured. Clearly, Dusty and I still have work to do.

"The whole postracial thing is confusing, isn't it?" I say.

We have just finished a discussion of *Huckleberry*

Finn, during which a few white students have described the frustration they experienced in high school classrooms with white teachers who refused to utter the word "nigger" when reading aloud from the book. Instead their teachers breezed past the word as if it weren't there. One young man says that he had to keep checking his pages as his teacher read. He wondered if his eyes had tricked him, and maybe the word wasn't really there on the page at all.

Dr. King's noble dream has degenerated into a cliché, a catchphrase, like "diversity," a way out of—as opposed to a way into—complex and textured conversations about race. At best, what the civil rights movement appears to have produced is a generation that is keen to look beyond race, but finds on the other side not freedom but a riddle. The riddle of race, something you see but must always pretend not to see.

Harrison, another one of my students, tells me that he saw me talking in the hallway with a guy he had played basketball with over the weekend but whose name he doesn't know. I ask Harrison to describe the guy. "He's tall," Harrison says. "He was wearing a yellow button-down shirt. He was carrying a blue backpack. It was around three thirty." And on like that.

A particular face comes to mind but I'm not sure. "Was he black?" I ask. Harrison falls silent and looks at me with horror in his eyes.

And then there is Katie, who, when she has cause to refer to me in class as a black woman, sends me an email afterward apologizing for referring to me as a black woman.

These days, what I encounter in the classroom is a generation afraid to say what they see.

I write back to Katie that it's okay, that I *am,* in fact, a black woman, and that whatever mistakes she imagines she is making when talking about race, I will, most likely, make them, too.

Maybe I see it too much. Maybe my vigilance separates me from my own family, none of whom, so far, feels the periodic need to be surrounded by brown skin as deeply I do. Why would they? Except for me, they have all grown up, or are growing up, in predominantly white environments.

In my room at the bed-and-breakfast, I talk with my daughters via our electronic devices. We show each other our respective mise-en-scènes. I turn the camera on my iPad toward an ornamental shoe, a white marble sculpture of a woman's head with a finger to its lips, and an old-fashioned typewriter. They are impressed by the bed, in particular its canopy of thin white silk.

I go to sleep and wake up to the purity of limited choices: the same few clothes, toiletries, books. I could do this, I think. I could live here. Maybe we would all be safer if I were on my own, away from the ones I love and could therefore hurt. I could stay here and not make any more mistakes. John could teach our daughters to live, and I could live here without saddling them with my past, my fears. But then, I quickly realize, I would not be able to touch them. I would no longer be able to feel the yielding texture of their skin when I pull them close, take their hands. This I could not abide.

. . .

Race is a social construction for which there is no scientific basis; racism is the foundation of that construction. I read and hear some version of these statements all the time; I repeat them in every course I teach. They are true. But when I am out in the world with my daughters, it is not a construction or its consequences that I fear will hurt them. What I fear are human beings, white human beings, who are not made of theory, but of flesh and blood.

I walk with Giulia and hold her hand. I cup it, wrap it with my own, and curve it into a tiny fist. I think about the killings, the routine destruction of brown bodies. *You're not taking her,* my hand says. *Not this one, not today.*

"I love you so much, I want to carry you around all day in my pocket," I tell Isabella, even though I am well aware of the fact that the same urge to protect her from harm would, if acted upon, result in her suffocation.

I want my children to breathe, to live and be free. Not only to experience the pleasure of their own skin but also the skin of others. I'm not sure if I have the language to teach them how, but this is what I want them to do.

White Friend

Love does not begin and end the way we seem to
think it does. Love is a battle, love is a war; love
is a growing up.

—James Baldwin

Grocery Store

Burlington, 2010. Karen and I stand talking in the middle
of a grocery store. We are talking about Len, her godson,
who is the son of a mutual friend. Karen is white; Len is
black. "This is the first time I've ever lived with a black
person," she tells me. Len has been living in her house for
almost a year.

The comment is not out of the blue. I have been telling Karen about a course I am teaching called Interracial
Intimacy, a course that speaks to one of my deepest beliefs,
which is that intimacy—shared space and time—is a crucial factor in improving race relations. I had described to
her an article I read about how few people of different races
spend time in each other's homes, in each other's company
in general.

Karen is sixty years old. She is slender and small, with
a narrow face and iron-straight blond hair. She has lived
in rural Vermont all of her life. The fact that she has never

lived with a black person before is not strange. According to the article, it would be strange if she *had* lived with a black person before, much less hosted one in her bathtub, which is where the conversation has taken us.

"The first time he took a bath there was a dark ring inside the tub!" Karen says, her eyes wide with revelation. She lives on a farm. It is Len's responsibility to take care of the animals.

She is waiting for a response, waiting for me to confirm this revelation. "Maybe he was just dirty," I offer. I don't say, *Our color, it doesn't come off.*

It's pretty clear to me that Karen realized the unsavoriness of her observation soon after it emerged from her mouth, but she couldn't stop herself from completing her train wreck of a thought. I know the feeling.

Karen leaves quickly to go back to her shopping. She tells me she's needed at home, maybe by Len, I think, who has perhaps since committed himself to cleaning the tub after he bathes. Good-bye, we say, see you soon.

Now I am standing alone in the middle of the grocery store, having forgotten why I came. I move furtively down aisles, my eyes scanning items without fully registering what they are, hoping not to see Karen again, sure she is just as carefully avoiding me. I want to laugh. Karen's confession is the most remarkable thing anyone has said to me in a long time, even more remarkable than the daily diet of odd and entertaining observations that my children share with my husband and me. John will be interested, too, but it's not him I want to tell—it's Loree.

"Did you tell her that it's not a stain?" Loree asks when I describe to her my encounter with Karen. We make a few more jokes like that. I had brought her the story like a gift, something to add to our growing trove of shared stories and experiences. But it's not working out like I planned; Loree's laugh is heavy, dark, and bitter. She has girlishly wavy flaxen blond hair and eyes as bright blue as a doll's. She trains her doll eyes on mine; her expression is opaque and serious. Clearly, she doesn't find this as funny as I do. She's more disgusted than amused.

"You're my only black friend," Loree told me recently.

Inheritance

I like to say that I inherited Loree from John because it usually makes people laugh. But it's true that Loree was part of John's human dowry, just like his biological family. And somewhere back there, remotely, intangibly, I inherited all of their history, the way they have indirectly inherited mine.

Loree and John are both from western Massachusetts. John grew up in Lenox, in the Berkshires, which became known in the Gilded Age as "the inland Newport" for its mansions, known quaintly as "cottages," summer homes for the wealthy. Loree, however, grew up on what amounted to the other side of the tracks, in Lenox Dale, a part of Lenox that was not featured in tourist brochures. When they were children, "the Dale," as it was known, was the kind of place that produced a kid like Anthony, who, John remembers, stole a car when he was in the third grade and beat his teacher with her own ruler.

Loree inherited me, too. Initially we were "John's friend" and "John's girlfriend," respectively, to each other, but a mutual affection grew quickly. What we admired first about each other was how much the other one loved John, who is more brother than friend to Loree. We loved the same man and we loved the same woman: John's mother, on whom Loree has modeled herself as a woman and a parent. But then we got to know each other, and on it went. This is the story Loree and I share with others when asked about the origins of our relationship.

But Loree has her own story that contains questions particular to being a white person with an only black friend. "Do I like you so much because you're black?" She has wondered about this, she tells me. "Would that make me a racist?"

Only Love

Like Loree and me, Karen and I share a love for the same woman. Her name is Estelle and she is Len's mother. She is black.

I have known Estelle for many years now; I met her within the first few months of arriving in Vermont. John picked her as a friend for me. They met on campus and struck up a lively conversation. "She's your kind of woman," he told me with some resentment. He knew what would happen, which is that I would take Estelle over, and we would develop the kind of friendship that women do when men aren't around.

Estelle is Karen's age, tall and strikingly beautiful. Whenever I see her, I am reminded of Janie Crawford in *Their Eyes Were Watching God*, whom another character describes as looking like her own daughter. Like Janie, Estelle sometimes wears blue jeans and her hair in a long braid. She walks with the confidence of someone who has found her place in the world. She is more sister than friend to me.

I like to look at Estelle. I like the strong, smooth timbre of her voice and the way she moves her hands when she talks. I like the warmth of her eyes and the dark, delicate freckles on her brown skin. Estelle's beauty is, for me, one of the benefits of our friendship, but is it actually the reason why I like her so much? If so, what does that make me?

John has great taste in friends for me; he knows the difference between what I like and what is good for me. It is largely because of him that the distance between what I like and what is good has collapsed over the last several years. My relationship with him and my children has, not surprisingly, changed the way I think about intimacy. I certainly ask different things of friendships now than I did when I was younger and childless; I ask more and I ask less. I used to want only friends who would fascinate me. Now I want friends who are kind. I used to want excitement, now I just want people to stick around.

An older friend told me that when she reached middle age, she took an inventory of the people in her life—family, friends old and new, neighbors, coworkers, even acquaintances—and decided that since it appeared she was stuck with them, she was just going to love them. After all, it's only love.

It is only love that Karen has to offer to Estelle's son. Maybe that is all anyone ever has to offer.

Camp Loree

For several years, my twin daughters spent a week during the summer on Loree's farm in southern Vermont. We called the week "Camp Loree." It is largely because of

Loree that my daughters have had the kind of Vermont experiences that inspire people to make pilgrimages here every summer. At Camp Loree, my daughters would ride horses and tend to the sheep that sometimes wandered into her home. During their week with her, the girls lazed in the middle of a lake in inner tubes. Loree would send me pictures of a beaming Isabella shoveling horse manure, and a radiant Giulia holding a bottle in the mouth of a baby lamb. When they leave home and people ask them what it was like to grow up in Vermont, I imagine that among other stories, my daughters will tell about the summer weeks they spent at Camp Loree.

Loree's Vermont is the Vermont of poetry and romance. Her home, a restored farmhouse that sits on five acres, neighbors a barn with a peace sign painted on its doors. The farmhouse is a precise reflection of Loree herself: unpretentious, imaginative, and casual; warm and inviting. Friends and family gather around a fireplace in a room with overstuffed couches that gently but persuasively pull your body in inch by inch until you are drowsy with warmth, good conversation, and the sun setting over the mountains outside of big bay windows. To the left is a kitchen in which rich dishes, both simple and complex, are conceived and then executed; where butter and jelly are coaxed into being. The winding wooden staircase is lined with photographs. Guests sleep under heavy, handmade quilts and wake to the bleating of sheep.

Loree's is the kind of home I imagined when I first pictured a life in Vermont, even though I knew I had neither the skill nor the drive to pull off that particular kind of Vermont life. The fact that Loree has made this home, its character and spirit, would inspire envy if Loree weren't the kind of person who finds envy tedious.

I admire Loree for the home she has made and for the mother that she is. Her children are grown, but they bear the mark of their mother's ingenuity and insights into the work of making one's way in the world.

I sent my children to southern Vermont in the summers not only to laze in inner tubes in lakes but also to benefit from the example of Loree and all that she knows. But there are things she doesn't know, like what it feels like to be the lone brown body among white ones, the small incidents of ignorance that can turn into scars that last a lifetime.

Once, as I am packing the girls up for Camp Loree, I realize that Loree might not know that my daughters need sunscreen; so many white people believe that the melanin in dark skin provides natural protection against sunburn.

I write Loree about the sunscreen. And then I write her about the experience of being black in a white place, what my children might experience, at the same time knowing that their childhood experiences are already so different from my own. Still, I ask her to be aware, always, of the fact that my daughters are vulnerable, brown bodies moving among people who rarely see dark skin.

I send the note and then worry for a bit. I consider what it would be like to receive such a message. Will Loree feel second-guessed, lectured at, or condescended to? Instead I am happy and relieved to discover that she is grateful for the information. And then she tells me that I am her only black friend.

Black Friend

Estelle is not my only black friend, but there was a long, lonely time during which I did not have many, and I was as conscious and careful when it came to the blackness of those few friends, perhaps, as Loree is when it comes to me. I expected to make black friends at college. I made a few, but I encountered divides of class, region, and temperament that proved as difficult to overcome as any racial barrier. I was finally in classes with people who looked like me, but they were nothing like me. They had gone to elite prep schools, belonged to exclusive clubs, and summered in places like the Berkshires, which may as well have been a foreign country to me back then. Ironically, it is only here in Vermont that I have a cohort of black friends in whose company I do not feel self-conscious. It is because and not in spite of the fact that we are among the few black people in this predominantly white place that we met and became close. Estelle and I made time to build a friendship in no small part because of race; we were drawn to each other for reasons both obvious and ineffable, it's true, but it is also true that we each wanted another black friend.

When I describe Camp Loree to Estelle, explain what it means to me and what I hope it will mean to my daughters, she nods. In many ways, what Loree offers my children is what Karen offers Len, which is a relationship with nature, something that I, a child of the suburbs, and Estelle, a child of the city, don't come by naturally. It is because of the essential values ingrained in the fabric and mundane details of the life she lives—this is why Estelle chose Karen for a godparent.

For two years, every time I saw Estelle I recalled Karen's grocery store revelation. One day, temptation took over, and I told her what Karen said about her son's skin. It was selfish, I knew, but my motive was not to create bad feelings between Estelle and Karen. Instead I wanted to understand what Estelle thought about the nature of love.

What I discovered, what I should have known, is that I didn't—couldn't—tell Estelle anything about Karen that she didn't already know. Still, I wanted to know why Karen merited such a sacred place in her life, particularly because Estelle once told me that she often finds herself wary of forming bonds with white people. So, why Karen? I asked her. She loves my child, she told me. She would do anything for him. She's family.

Is family what we call friends whom we love beyond measure? Or is it just what we call people we have decided, for whatever reason, that we're stuck with?

The Look

After one particular week of Camp Loree, John and I met Loree, her husband, and our daughters at an artisanal pizza restaurant halfway between Manchester and Burlington. We had a pleasant lunch and then got up to leave. On the way out, Loree glanced at a woman at a table near us. Her doll eyes darkened. She walked forward but kept her head turned in the woman's direction.

"Did you see that?" Loree asked me. "Did you see how she was looking at the girls?"

I turned to look at the woman. She didn't look particularly friendly or unfriendly. She talked to the man sitting across from her as she ate a salad. She had thinning blond hair and wore a fine gold bracelet on her wrist.

I knew where this was going, having been there before with other white friends, the ones who see racism everywhere, hiding like a burglar behind potted plants in restaurants when I'm just trying to eat lunch in peace.

When we reached the car, we were still talking about the woman in the restaurant. Loree was convinced that she had a disapproving look in her eyes as they took in my brown daughters. I was convinced that Loree was wrong. I *wanted* Loree to be wrong. I didn't want the afternoon to be spoiled by a reminder of the ugliness in the world.

I understood that what Loree meant to do was show me that we were in this ugly world together. But the effect was to remind me of the vulnerability that stalks me, my helplessness to protect my children from the little nicks that may gather into scars like the ones I carry.

Later, Loree and I would discuss that moment, the underlying conflict between our interpretations of the woman's look. Loree reminded me that a few years earlier, I had told her a story about experiencing racial hatred directed at me and my daughters. It happened on Martha's Vineyard while we were swimming in a hotel pool. That hatred was conveyed through a long, unblinking stare that made me tremble with fear. As a result of that story, Loree had developed a sensitivity to looks. It was what I had asked her to do.

I am intrigued when Loree tells me that I am her only black friend. What's that like? I ask her. What is the hardest part of having an only black friend?

"The hardest part for me now is me," she says. She

worries that her experience of growing up white in a racist world might prevent her from ever being able to see beyond race when it comes to our friendship. She worries that her own self-consciousness might compromise the integrity of our bond.

Maybe the hardest part of having an only black friend is Loree herself and her self-consciousness when it comes to the racial difference between us. But Loree has another problem, and the problem is the particular black friend she has chosen, or that has been chosen for her.

Because this particular black friend thinks about race all of the time sometimes, but just as often not at all. I want to talk about it, and I don't. I want my white friend to be aware of racism, and at the same time I don't want to be reminded of racism. I laugh at gaffes about dark rings in bathtubs, yet I shudder with anger and sorrow when I think of all the dangers, large and small, implicit and explicit, from which I will not be able to protect my daughters. These contradictions may be a function of the condition of blackness, or they may be evidence of the quirks in my personality—it's hard to say. It must be tricky terrain, the experience of being a white friend with an only black friend, and there is no road map.

But there is one certainty: we are, sometimes joyfully, sometimes frustratingly, stuck with each other, white friend and black friend. Let's call it love.

Her Glory

Isabella asks me if she can get her hair straightened, or flattened, as she calls it. When curiosity outdistances my good judgment, I comply. In order to maximize the potential for drama inherent in the occasion, we schedule the flattening for a few days before her birthday. Giulia agrees to accompany Isabella for moral support, and also because Tamara, her hairdresser, always has Popsicles in her freezer. Three hours after I drop the girls off, I receive a summons to retrieve them.

The warm, thick smells of coconut and shea butter greet me as I enter the apartment. Giulia and Tamara's son lean into each other on a black leather couch, transfixed by the television. Isabella sits on a stool with her back to me while Tamara stands in front of her, tidying the hair on either side of Isabella's face.

I walk slowly around my daughter's head. Crystal Gayle and Cousin It from *The Addams Family* come to mind. Isabella's hair is long and smooth and shines a glossy blue-black, like Veronica's hair in the Archie comics. My little girl is gone. In her place has emerged the head of celebrities and freaks and cartoon characters.

Tamara keeps a small black comb tucked into her crossed arms and watches me circle the stranger on the stool. Isabella ignores me as I examine her head from every angle. Along with the other kids, she is absorbed in *The Cosby Show,* an episode in which Cliff puts together a funeral for Rudy's dead goldfish.

Isabella's hair isn't a goldfish. It is a glass catfish, an Aulonocara Firefish, a Sunshine Peacock. Like any exotic pet, it will need careful tending. Specifically, Tamara tells me, it will have to be wrapped into a beehive, which should then be covered by a silk scarf before bed. She demonstrates the steps a few times and then hands me the pet. She tries to coach me through it, but I can't maintain control over the straight, slippery mass. "That's not bad," Tamara reassures me as I transform her sweeping crown of a beehive into a loosely bound radish. "Just do the best you can," she says.

It starts to rain. Giulia and I lift my jacket like a canopy and run alongside Isabella to the car. Once we are safely inside, the three of us examine our new pet, relieved to see that it is still snugly and silkily affixed to Isabella's head. We congratulate one another on a job well done. But then I remember that it is supposed to rain the next day, too, which will be accompanied by humidity, which will lead to sweating. I have fulfilled Isabella's greatest wish, but it comes with the attendant costs of girlhood—black girlhood, to be precise. If we keep it flattened, she will come to worry over weather reports and view the elements as enemies. What a mistake, I think, as I glance at her extraordinary head in the rearview mirror.

My daughters were nearly bald when I first met them. In Northern Ethiopia it is customary to keep the heads of girl babies shorn during the first year of their lives in the hopes that regular clippings will ensure long hair in the future. My husband and I loved our daughters' bald heads, especially the way they made their eyes seem even bigger than they actually were. For the first two years of their lives I kept their hair cut close to their scalps. Around that time, however, a nagging thought began to take root, a sentiment I had grown up hearing all my life: girls should have long hair. I started to sense judgment beneath the questions of people who asked why I kept the girls' hair so short. As dazzling as I found my bald-headed babies, and as much as I resented the straitjacket of conventional beauty standards, particularly when it comes to black girls, the thought, once rooted, bloomed quickly.

Isabella did not object when I embarked upon the project of growing her hair. Now, after ten years, her hair has been my longest-lasting hobby since I gave up collecting stamps in high school. Her hair is my garden, and I have pruned and weeded her head as ardently as my mother used to tend to her flowers and plants. It's gone through many phases. The first, a short, fluffy Afro, became untenable as tangles began to develop just as quickly as her hair grew. I thought short braids would keep her hair neat and orderly, but even after several YouTube tutorials, I could only manage to produce lumpy, uneven knots. I found a young woman with swift, nimble fingers who told me that extensions would help Isabella's hair grow faster. Even though I suspected this was only a myth, I consented; I figured she knew what she was doing.

The extension phase didn't last long. The time and expense became a nuisance, and I was eager to take over the principal role in the saga of Isabella's hair care. After a brief stint as a feathery ball on top of her head, her hair became long enough for box braids, which require the hair first to be divided into box-like sections and braided. The box braid stage was my favorite. I got so skilled at parting that her entire head resembled a map of small Midwestern states. As I combed her hair, I studied its range of textures; some strands felt like tumbleweeds and others like corn silk. I came to know the landscape of her scalp—with its mysterious valleys, bumps, and dents—more intimately than I know my own.

After a long week of teaching, the braiding was private and meditative. Once we had negotiated the time (midafternoon was ideal), place (the living room), and the appropriate distraction (television), I enjoyed gathering the instruments and potions necessary to bring her tired, fraying braids back to life. I took as much pride in watching my own braiding skills develop as I did in my daughter's growing mane. Unlike teaching, braiding was labor that had tangible results, and labor it was. I complained proudly about the way my back ached after hours of bending over Isabella's head. When I referred to them as "our" braids, she didn't correct me.

The rhythm of braiding was calming—until it wasn't. No matter how gently I tried to perform the task, there was always, eventually, screaming. After the screaming, there was whining, because no matter how early I started, I found myself constantly racing against bedtime. If we were lucky, the Discovery Channel delivered her favorite narcotic, *Animal Planet*. Isabella would sit with her hands folded in her lap, absorbed in displays of humans being mauled by alligators.

These are among my happiest memories: the small, still, folded brown hands; the immeasurable feeling of triumph after calming dry, angry knots into shiny, peace-loving strands while the accompanying music to the *Maneaters* documentary series played in the background. I cherished the alone time with Isabella, who at that point in her life considered it her job to keep track of the growing list of my maternal failings. But she always approved of my braiding. I would wait excitedly for her regal nod after she studied her fresh braids in the mirror from every possible angle. Eventually, we switched from box braids to cornrows. It was then that Tamara entered our lives. I said I was relieved to have my afternoons back, but privately, I grieved. My hands felt useless, the evenings barren. I busied myself with laundry while I replayed my Greatest Untangling Hits in my mind, like the knot that brought tears to my eyes before I conquered it after an hour of microsurgical separation.

The road to perfect cornrows was painful; Isabella called them "hurting braids." They involved more tugging and tightening than box braids.

"Don't cry," Tamara would command as she pulled her comb through Isabella's hair and braided away. Having worked on the heads of many children, Tamara was unmoved by Isabella's discomfort. But I had to turn away when I saw my daughter scrunch her tiny features and make miniature fists, determined not to cry, even while fat tears rolled down her cheeks anyway. But as hard as it was to watch, I never once told Tamara to stop.

I attended only the first session of the hurting braids. With every tug of Tamara's comb, Isabella took my hand and squeezed my fingers until I imagined I could hear bones cracking. I embraced the pain; I deserved it. After tiring of the silent drama going on between Isabella and me, Tamara forbade me to hang around during appointments.

The only time John accompanied Isabella to Tamara's, Isabella insisted that he stay with her. She had her father, a former hockey player, arrange his big body on the floor at her feet and hold her tiny hand for three hours while Tamara wrestled with her hair. John came home shaken. "Does the Geneva Convention know about this?" he asked.

Giulia witnessed enough of her sister's braiding sessions to conclude that long hair wasn't worth the pain. She didn't falter in her conviction, even when she was mistaken for a boy; even when, after a particularly sweaty afternoon on the playground, the class troublemaker said that her hair made her look like Albert Einstein. "Einstein is a *genius*," she told me. "So the joke's on him."

My father was not impressed by Giulia's fortitude. He grumbled about her hair during our trips to Nashville. "Braids or *something*," he pleaded with me during one visit, nodding his head in the direction of Giulia, who perched on her knees and colored on a piece of paper next to him. The longer Giulia's hair stayed short, the more my father worried. "What's happening with Giulia's hair?" he said once on the phone in response to "Hi, Dad." Suddenly, I was sixteen years old again, pained at having been the cause of his displeasure, and furious at myself for caring.

"Giulia likes her hair short," I told him, my heart racing.

"She's a little girl," he snapped. "She doesn't know what she wants." He offered to pay so that I could take her to a proper beauty salon.

Giulia was five years old. How ridiculous, I thought, as I picked up my child early from kindergarten in order to make her appointment at a beauty shop. But I needed help. As much as Isabella disliked her hair being pulled and stroked by combs and brushes, she endured it. Giulia, on the other hand, made for the door whenever she glimpsed a hair-styling instrument headed in her direction. "It's just basic grooming," I tried to reason with her as she darted around the room. Sometimes I held firm and forced a pick through her curls even when doing so required me to physically restrain her. But more and more I resorted to some superficial sculpting with my palms on her way out the door. There were a few mornings when I told her just to put on a hat.

I didn't realize how far from grace we had fallen until the stylist at the beauty salon gave me a look that was so offended and alarmed that it was easy to conjure an image of her dialing Child Protective Services. Her alarm linked arms with my guilt. I looked at Giulia, whom I had sworn to protect. My job was also to serve as a custodian of her beauty, was it not? I had failed, and not only as a mother, but even worse, as a black mother. My lovely child's disorganized head had exposed me as an imposter, a pretender. A white mother's inexperience with her black daughter's hair might have been forgivable, but I was supposed to know better. I bowed my head. Giulia and I left the store with bags full of treacly hair-care products, all of them bearing the name of the salon. Those bottles, half empty, lined the bottom of the cabinet under the bathroom sink for several years, until I finally threw them out.

When my mother died, I decided to cut my own hair; I wanted to wear my grief. I was living in New Haven at the time, but the stylist I had seen as a college student was out of the question. I pictured Mr. Jacques—tall, black, and as sharp as a barber's blade—and his look of scorn at even the suggestion that I would cut my hair. I saw him only for occasional trims, which he deigned to execute only after scolding me. "God gave you all this hair," he muttered once while poking at the ends with tiny scissors. He reminded me of where I came from, so I kept seeing him. For the purpose of mourning my mother, though, I chose a stranger—a white stranger. The stylist I chose was tall and blond and did not question me or ask me what my parents would think. She moved my head from side to side, her shears cocked and loaded.

"More?" she kept asking as she steadily clipped her way around my head.

"Yes!" I was exhilarated. But after she was finished and I saw that most of my hair had disappeared, I cried.

I got used to my short hair. Then, I came to love it. Then, I forgot about it. I had acclimated completely to my new hair when a cousin commented on Facebook that my short hair enhanced my resemblance to my father. I was pleased by the comment and imbued it with larger, symbolic meanings. My short hair may have started out as a memorial to my mother, I thought, but it had come to represent the peace that had settled between my father and me in the wake of her death. I told my father, thinking he would feel the same. He did not. "Girls should look like their mothers," he said, leaning on the first and last words to make sure I understood.

My mother had what is known as "good hair" in the black vernacular. Her hair rituals were simple, but when I was a child, I found them glamorous. I sat as close as I could while she gathered a bouquet of her hair and pulled a plastic teal-blue comb through it all the way to its fine ends. When I asked if I could comb it, she said no, and waved my eager hands away. As a child, her straight hair had exposed her to envy and adoration from family and strangers. It had excited jealous cruelty in people she loved and unsettling reverence from those she didn't. She did not want me to fall under its spell.

At the beginning and end of each day, my mother wore her hair in a loose braid. But before she left the house in the morning, she wound it into a bun that she fixed in place with large hairpins. Over the years, my mother talked idly about cutting her hair, but she never once even trimmed it. She kept her glory intact, but she kept it out of sight.

"Cut your hair, lose your glory" is what my mother heard growing up in the Bible Belt. The saying derives from a passage in 1 Corinthians: "If a woman have long hair, it is a glory to her: for her hair is given her for a covering." My grandmother cut her hair once when my mother was young. "If I had wanted a woman with short hair, I would have married one," my grandfather told her. So she grew it back. For most of my life, my grandmother kept her hair coiled in a braided bun just like my mother, taking it down only to wash and comb it.

When it was long, my own hair was too abundant for buns, and no combs or hairpins could tame it. In middle school, I tried braiding it at bedtime like my mother, hoping that the restraint would force my hair into docility by morning, but my hair was willful and quickly revived itself after a night in captivity. I slathered on creams and pomades to keep it small and close to my head, but my hair had big dreams and wanted to know the world. When I entered high school, I tried straightening it myself with a flatiron, but no matter how much heat I applied, the frizzy bits at my temples could not be subdued. All the while, I cut out photographs of black models and actresses with bone-straight hair. They looked happy and confident. If I had hair like theirs, I assumed, the rest would be mine, too. I remember one picture of a model taken against a white background, as if her hair and clothes were all there was to her life. I believed that if I could get my hair perfectly straight, I wouldn't have to worry about it, or any of my other teenage problems, anymore.

Even though my mother thought it was a waste of money and foolish, to boot, somehow I convinced her to allow me to get my hair relaxed when I was sixteen. There is nothing relaxing about a relaxer. You lie back in a sink for endless minutes while the sodium hydroxide sets in. The deeper the burning sensation, the more successful the process. Once your hair is relaxed, you're not allowed to scratch for an agonizing three days. Give in to the itch and burn your scalp. I could never be faithful to the mandate not to scratch, so I eventually gave up on the relaxer and surrendered to my natural hair texture, but not happily. Once my mother pointed to a Donna Summer album cover that featured the singer's face surrounded by long curly locks. "You have hair like this girl," my mother said. I burst into tears right there in the record store. I went back to bands and barrettes.

"What are you afraid of?" asked a friend of my parents, a professor at a local university, a black woman with short, natural hair. "Why do you bind your hair?" It was fellowship hour at church. We were standing side by side, each of us holding identical Styrofoam cups. I held mine tighter and then looked for the first moment to excuse myself. She was right; I was afraid. It was not until college that I gathered the courage to free my hair. Once I did, I shuddered to realize that what I had been afraid of was simply being black.

A psychologist shows a young African American girl a row of cartoon dolls whose skin colors range from paper-white to deep mahogany. The dolls are identical in every other way. All are poised mid-skip with enormous smiles that reach, literally, from ear to ear. Their short dresses are the color of hospital scrubs. So are the bows in their hair, which is styled like the comb of a cartoon rooster. The girl being interviewed wears her straightened hair in sleek ponytails on either side of her head.

"Who is better? Smarter? Prettier?" the psychologist asks her. After a moment of consideration, the girl picks one of the dolls on the lighter end of the spectrum.

I freeze the screen on the frame of the array of dolls

and call my daughters into the room. "They're all beauti-ful," Isabella says gently, looking at me with concern, as if I have, to her sadness, missed this important life lesson. Giulia picks the darkest cartoon doll. I ask her why. "She looks the most like me," she explains.

The interview is a scene from the 2011 documentary *Dark Girls*. The test is a modern version of the Clark Doll Test, created in 1939 by Kenneth and Mamie Clark, in which black and white children were presented with dolls whose skin was either deep brown or pale pink and asked which one was smarter, prettier, and better behaved. Overwhelmingly, children of both races chose the white doll. The Clarks determined that racial segregation played a key factor in negative attitudes toward dark skin. The Clark Doll Test was entered as evidence in the landmark 1954 case *Brown v. Board of Education*.

When is a doll just a doll? Soon after we brought our daughters home from Ethiopia, the parents of a close friend came to visit. They had known me for most of my adult life and had anticipated the girls' arrival as impa-tiently as anyone else. They brought with them a pink plas-tic doll in a pink terrycloth onesie with plastic blond hair and dull blue eyes. As I recounted stories of the weeks we spent in Ethiopia waiting to become parents, I held the doll tenderly. After all, it was a gift from people who loved me, offered to my daughters only in love.

For a long time, this was the only doll the girls wanted to play with. But ultimately it wound up with their other dolls in the same graveyard: the potter's field in the back of their closet, where other once-cherished plastic bodies were discarded after cruel amputations and rough, ragged haircuts. During a routine purging, I found their beloved pink doll in the same state, its dull blue eyes tattooed with a rainbow of crayons.

I said nothing to my daughters about the pink doll; I saw no harm in it. I said nothing either when, at a university event, my daughters rushed to Rose, a friend and former babysitter, and stood on either side of her head, gathering and dividing her long, blond hair, braiding and unbraiding it. Rose looked at me with compassion. She is insightful and sensitive when it comes to the tangled relationship between race and beauty. Neither one of us wanted Giulia and Isabella to lose themselves in Rose's hair; neither one of us wanted to make them feel ashamed for doing so. Here was a human being whom they loved, a young woman whose hair was long and blond and therefore enviable in a culture that valorizes such attributes. But this enviable hair belonged to Rose, whose every attribute they adored in equal measure. It was not her hair they loved, but Rose, I told myself, and watched my daughters' eyes radiate with wonder as they weaved their brown hands in and out of Rose's blond hair. It pleased me to see their joy. I didn't realize I was holding my breath until they lost interest in Rose's hair and went to spend time with other friends.

I describe the scene with my daughters and Rose to my friend Estelle, and we puzzle over it together. Estelle's children are adults, each one long and lean. When they are in public, the eyes of strangers light upon them and stay there. They are black but their skin is light, ranging in color from bronze to light cedar. Estelle told me that when they were young, she rarely told them they were beautiful. It was because of their skin color; she never wanted them to associate light skin with beauty.

I tell my daughters they are beautiful every day, sometimes several times a day. I believe that what I am doing has an important purpose. I believe that, brick by brick, compliment by compliment, I am building a fortress against the world out there that, studies show, will judge them as inferior for their dark skin. I want to create a running script in their heads, a narrative extolling the particular beauty of their dark skin, should they encounter such discrimination. But I also do this because they *are*, indeed, beautiful, so when my daughters tell me I am being superficial, this is true, too.

As superficial as it may be, I take my daughters on pilgrimages to Washington, D.C., Nashville, and New York in order to enjoy the spectacle of blackness. Visiting my father and brothers in Brooklyn over Christmas, Giulia, Isabella, and I find a bench on a street with a row of hip restaurants. We sip smoothies and watch the women who walk our way. There is a girl with a copper-colored Afro so bright it glitters. Here is a woman with a crown of braids that look as smooth as whipped butter. Another one has extensions down to her waist, the tips flaming red. We smile and look and sometimes, frankly, stare. I am grateful that the day is bright and clear, a perfect backdrop to all of this glory.

We all wearied of the exotic pet atop Isabella's head sooner than I would have predicted. Giulia said I shouldn't have gotten her sister's hair flattened at all. "She's been a brat about it ever since," she said. Giulia had put all of her diplomatic talents to work in order to have a chance to play with Isabella's hair. She bribed her twin with toys, money, and promises to be her "servant" for a day. Isabella accepted all the treasures and promises and then yanked her head away from Giulia just as she began to stroke the pet. She was never able to get her hands deep into its coat.

Giulia was right. Instead of Isabella, I had brought home from Tamara's apartment a beautiful, obnoxious monster that now cackled as she ran away from her sister who stood with comb and brush aloft. The same creature tossed her Breck Girl hair in the mirror and told her reflection stories in sentences that traveled up into question marks at the end, just like a Valley Girl. It didn't take long for Isabella herself to become bored of these routines. She asked to get her hair braided again.

Tamara and I scheduled an appointment just before my daughters and I made a trip to Nashville to visit my father. When I called to firm up plans, I told him about our adventures in hair flattening. Instead of making his usual inquiry into the length and style of Giulia's hair, he asked me if I'd watched the Oscars. In particular he wanted to know if I had seen Lupita Nyong'o onstage after winning Best Supporting Actress for her role in the 2013 movie *12 Years a Slave*. I knew immediately that what he really wanted to talk about was Nyong'o's short hair.

"She's a beautiful woman," my father said. "Her hairstyle reminds me of Giulia."

Giulia reminds me of my grandmother. Because at the age of eighty-nine, my grandmother, then a widow for four decades, had her hair cut all the way up to her chin. She just got tired of messing with it, she said.

Motherland

"We've got a pair of twins. You want 'em?" Helen barks into the phone at two a.m. She is loud, as usual. I can hear her through the pillow I'm pressing against my ears. John whispers firmly that we will call her in the morning. It is August. We are at a hotel in Quebec City, on a vacation to celebrate my birthday. I sit up and lean back against the headboard. It is strange, terrifying, and simple: life, as we have been living it, is over.

Helen is our American adoption liaison. We met her a year before under a pavilion in a tiny town in Vermont. The occasion was a reunion, of sorts, a gathering of families that Helen had created. She wore a long, vibrant, shapeless dress patterned with flowers in purple, pink, and blue. She tipped her head back and laughed at something. Her body jiggled when she laughed; the folding chair in which she sat wobbled and struggled to keep her in place. Next to her, two obese white women fussed over a toddler with skin the color of caramel.

I approached Helen slowly, my pace disproportionate to the rapid thrumming of my heart. I did not want to appear too eager. I had given careful thought to how I should present myself at this moment, from the speed of my gait to my wardrobe. I chose a layered silk dress in avocado green, a friendly color, I thought. I wore a small straw hat that I thought made me look playful, and dainty gold sandals that I hoped projected the aura of fairy tales.

"Are you Helen Franklin?" I asked her, knowing very well that she was. Anyone who was interested in adopting children from Ethiopia did so through Helen. Breathless stories about her charisma and savvy circulated among people who were friends of friends of friends with Ethiopian children whose adoptions were made possible by Helen.

Like all entrepreneurs, pioneers, and megalomaniacs, Helen liked to tell stories of her success. Her mission began when an Ethiopian friend explained the difficulty of finding homes for children who had been orphaned in the war between Ethiopia and Eritrea. Helen took on the cause. Local agencies told her she would fail, that white families in Vermont would not adopt black children.

"I put an ad in the paper and I had a hundred calls by morning," she told me as we sat next to each other at a picnic table. I had no way of knowing if this was true, but I liked what it said about Vermont, and about Helen. I sat with my back straight and hands folded. I was trying to think of something clever to say when Helen was called away to meet other prospective parents.

I stood up to find John, who was talking to a white man and a black woman, husband and wife. Their two teenage Ethiopian daughters wore bathing suits under their sundresses. They looked hopefully at the lake where children much younger than they were swam and played. Their father was bespectacled and balding, well into middle age. I was drawn to his soft, kind air. His wife, tall, stately, and American, wandered off to examine the potluck offerings. The man's daughters made their boredom plain; one of them leaned her forehead on his shoulder and sighed loudly as John and her father laughed and traded Vermont stories. *Teenagers*, I thought, and sighed a little myself. The father looked at me and mouthed slowly, "This is great." I wasn't sure if he meant being the father of this bored, beautiful teenager, being an adoptive father, or being a father at all. But it didn't matter. The joy on his face was pure, as if he himself were a child and experiencing for the first time one of the world's elemental delights: love.

It had felt like an audition but it wasn't. Helen had decided to help us before she even met us. She had heard about us through friends of friends, the same way we had learned of her. She kept us in thrall for long months with stories of how she had turned hopeful couples into parents. She was working overtime for us, she insisted. But then weeks would pass without a word from her.

"What about Burundi?" she asked one day when she finally returned a phone call. She wasn't one to waste words, not even *hello*.

My stomach dropped. "We never talked about Burundi," I said and tried to push back a creeping image of Helen with closed eyes sticking pins randomly into a map of Africa.

"Maybe she'll start making up countries," I said to John when he came home. We both laughed distractedly. At first we had called Helen's coarse manner and unpredictable ways harmless, but the deeper in we got with her, the harder it became to view her through that lens. We were no longer charmed. Instead we began to experience an ominous sensation that something was wrong, like climbers slowly losing purchase on a rope. Ironically, perhaps, the more uneasy we became, the more desperately we clung to Helen and her promises. She had helped so many others, we reasoned. It would all surely work out in the end.

But today in Quebec City, there is no angst, only joy. I shower and dress, conscious of every movement: the future is happening now. Mundane activities take on tremendous significance. I brush and floss rigorously but carefully. I pull my shoelaces taut and double lace them. I am almost a mother; it's time to start setting examples.

John and I have breakfast near our hotel and then take a walk through the Joan of Arc Garden in Battlefields Park. Brilliant formations of sunflowers, freesia, and daisies line the path on the way to the bronze statue of the French warrior and saint. The sun shines ecstatically. In Ethiopia, it is the rainy season.

The twins are eight months old and do not have names, only nicknames. We discuss possibilities.

"I always wanted a daughter named Julia," I tell him, "after my aunt."

"How about with the Italian spelling?" So, Julia becomes Giulia.

"Okay, and then Elizabeth." I blame my father for my penchant for British names. We agree on Isabella, another Italian variation of a name I love. John's musical passions determine our choices of middle names. Giulia gets Naima, after the John Coltrane ballad. For Isabella, we choose Pannonica, after Pannonica "Nica" de Koenig-swarter, the bebop baroness without whose patronage the careers of Charlie Parker, Thelonious Monk, and others would have taken a different course. Bernard and Gennari will be third and last names, respectively.

"Those are big names for little girls," a friend says when I tell her, and I imagine the names balanced on the tiny torsos of the babies in the photograph Helen emailed to us. They can't walk or speak words, but their stories are already as mighty as mountains. To us, the names are melodious and sublime, but what is most attractive to me is the collision of cultures and histories they represent. *Welcome to your lives with us.* I send the thought flying across the Atlantic.

The rules concerning independent adoptions in Ethiopia have recently become more stringent, we discover along the way. We find this out not from Helen, but from an American agency that has hired her. The agency is proficient in Chinese adoptions, but they are new to Africa. In fact, we are part of their pilot program. We contact the agency ourselves after Helen becomes more and more difficult to reach. When she does return our calls, she is dodgy, giving us vague answers to basic questions about what to expect in Ethiopia. The agency hired Helen because of her experience with Ethiopian bureaucracy, but the director quickly tires of her imperious manner and unwillingness to follow protocol. In fact, when John and I contact Marjorie, the agent assigned to our case, we discover she has never heard of us. Helen has kept our case a secret, most likely because the adoption scenario she has designed for us is, at best, irregular. The agency fires Helen and cautions us not to communicate with her anymore. The problem is, they don't know anything about our case, which, though irregular, is not illegal. Because they want their program to succeed, and because they want to help us, they decide that we should go along with Helen's plan, which is to arrange a meeting right away between us and the twins' maternal family.

It is impossible not to maintain contact with Helen. She is enraged by her termination. The real reason she was fired, she tells us, is because the agency is corrupt. The director went to Ethiopia to buy babies, Helen insists, but she intervened. As revenge against her, she explains, Yonas, the Ethiopian liaison to the agency, is trying to sabotage our adoption. In November, she hands down an ultimatum: we must sever ties with the agency if we want to become parents to the twins.

It is impossible to reconcile Helen's bizarre tale of crime and general villainy with the kind, helpful, and utterly transparent communications we have received from the agency. It is impossible to heed either party's advice, which is to cease contact with the other one. It is possible only to get out of bed in the morning, eat lunch at lunchtime, and remember, as I wash dishes, that my feet are on solid ground. I sit down to write and try to ration the moments in which I call up the picture of the girls on my computer. When I do, I try to resist the urge to think very deeply about the curve of their feet and the brilliance of their eyes. This, too, proves impossible. I tell the agency the truth, that I cannot turn away from Helen, and I lie to Helen and swear that I have broken with the agency. Helen, my anvil, my savior. Just as Tea Cake says of his lover Janie in *Their Eyes Were Watching God,* she holds the keys to the kingdom.

In the meantime, John and I pack. We pack receiving blankets, wipes, pacifiers, bottles, clothes, and toys. We pack flashlights, a first-aid kit, and granola bars. In between the necessities, we wedge in a portable DVD player and three seasons of the HBO series *The Wire*. (We don't consider the impracticality of these items until months later, when we have arrived back in the States and our daughters are safely and legally ours.) We ask Marjorie if we should bring diapers.

"Don't worry. You can find them anywhere," says the director. She is wrong about this, and much else.

In Addis Ababa, we are met by Yonas, the Ethiopian liaison of the agency, a gentle man with a slim, handsome face and a small, tidy beard. We are soothed by the sight of him; he projects confidence and calm. I decide not to think too deeply about the darkly comic game of espionage in which he immediately involves us. If we see Helen, who has been in Addis for months, we are to feign innocence while engineering conversations designed to reveal her whereabouts and activities in the city. Yonas helps us collect our bags, peering over the top of his tinted eyeglasses as he scans the terminal, which is sparsely populated with worn-out, slow-moving travelers. They are wonderful, these travelers, yawning luxuriously, hoisting bags elegantly onto carts, and lining up casually at currency exchange windows. I imagine myself as one of them, as if I, too, were going about unremarkable business on an unremarkable day in the capital city of Ethiopia.

Across the room, I see Aster, a woman I met on the

plane. She was asleep, shrouded in a large white shawl, when I gave her seat an inadvertent bump while trying to stuff my bag into the compartment above her. She graciously excused me and we talked across the aisle during the fourteen-hour flight.

She and her twin sister run an import-export business. They own a textile factory in Addis, which manufactures blankets and clothing made of the same fine, hand-woven cotton that embraced her body. She leaned over to let me finger the soft, willowy cloth, called *gabi*, which is used in Ethiopia for clothing, shawls, and blankets. The baubles on her gold charm bracelet rang like tiny church bells as she showed me the edge of the fabric, threaded in the gold and blue of fine jewels. Our fingers nearly touched. Hers extended into shapely nails painted a subdued plum. She invited me to come and see her factory and meet her twin sister.

"Do you like being a twin?" I asked.

"We have our moments." She smiled.

Her daughter is a student at Amherst College. When Aster returns to the States, she will bring blankets made of *gabi* for her and her roommates, as her daughter requested. We talked about daughters and mothers and sisters until our stories got shorter and our sentences sparser. After one more exchange, Aster said softly, "I'll see you when we land."

I chat with Aster while Yonas tells John the details of the plan the agency has concocted for us to be able to meet (soon-to-be-called-if-all-goes-well) Giulia and Isabella swiftly and with no interference from Helen. First, we will visit the agency's foster home, where the twins will be staying until the adoption is finalized. We will have some time to spend in Addis before we must return to the airport to make a flight to Mekele, the capital city in the Northern Tigray region, which will be followed by a three-hour drive to Adigrat. In the desert well beyond the city, the girls and their extended family are waiting.

Yonas whistles and waves and a dark-green Fiat pulls up to the curb. The driver, Eleazar, will ferry us around Addis for the duration of our stay, which is supposed to last only a week. Eleazar has large, smoky eyes and a sharply planed face. His blue jeans are crisp; his white linen shirt is lightly, elegantly rumpled. He is as calm as a glass of tap water while the city buzzes frantically on the other side of the car doors. The golden day is overcast with exhaust and dirt. We pass shanties and tall buildings in early stages of existence, their steel bodies framed by wooden scaffolding, like halo braces worn by people with spine injuries. Eleazar rests his elbow on the car door as he drives. At a stoplight, he chats with a child who wears a drawer full of candy strapped around his neck, like a 1940s cigarette girl. The boy is dusty everywhere except his teeth, which are strong-looking and even. He squints at us, foreigners even more foreign than this classic Italian car that, we soon learn, is ubiquitous in Addis. I wave at the boy and he waves back tentatively. Eleazar laughs a little, and then turns back to resume his deft weaving in and out of the congested city traffic.

"My Africa, Motherland of the Negro peoples!" declaims Langston Hughes in his 1940 autobiography *The Big Sea*.

As a very young man, he worked on a ship that eventually docked in Dakar. "And me a Negro! Africa! The real thing, to be touched and seen, not merely read about in a book."

I had never dreamed of Africa, not once entertained fantasies of an innate bond between me and the continent, not like other African Americans I know or have read about who believe in a primordial tie that links them to the motherland, one as pure as placenta and persistent as the connective tissue that keeps the body's organs in place. But as I stand holding the pole on the shuttle to the plane that will take us to Mekele, I feel I am in the middle of something, something bigger than myself, but in which I am somehow *involved*. I am surprised and pleased when people speak to me in Amharic, the way I seem to blend in, though that presumption of compatriotism doesn't last long. My Americanness is all over me, beneath language, down to the way I laugh and move my hands. My Americanness is *in* me, too, in the assumptions I brought with me of which I was not even aware, assumptions about an "Africa" gleaned from news reports: famine, poverty, war. That version of Africa directly contradicts what I see around me: men and women lost in thought, sitting and standing in this short, accordion-like shuttle, a small waiting plane, mountains as distant as memories, a landscape both dignified and ordinary. This is the real thing, to be touched and seen. Upon boarding the plane, people talk in low voices through the airline attendant's lecture on seat belts and emergency exits. Turn off your cell phones, stow your tray tables. I close my eyes as we take off.

. . .

We meet Girma and Berhanu, our driver and translator, respectively, in the Mekele airport. The sun is already setting as we load ourselves and all of our bags into the Land Rover that will take the four of us to Adigrat.

John holds the handrail inside the jeep and talks to the men. From Ethiopian culture, politics, and art, their conversation winds into American music; John praises a new favorite jazz musician, while Berhanu and Girma talk about the country music singers they like. Hank Williams Jr.'s woeful voice pours out of the speakers, followed by Norah Jones. In my hands, I hold small, square, black-and-white photographs of Giulia and Isabella. In these particular photographs, in this particular light, they look Siberian to me, with their ruddy cheeks and oval eyes. I tuck the pictures back into my purse. The hills around us appear dense and stubborn against a sky quickly fading from gray to white to black. A VW bus passes us, then what looks like an army tank. A shepherd leads a camel carrying saddlebags of salt as big and fat as barrels. The brush on the side of the road appears to thicken as the road narrows. Girma turns the radio dial to a station playing songs in Amharic. I open my purse and touch the pictures. I pray I will be good enough.

The four of us have dinner in an Adigrat hotel where we will be spending the night. We sit close together at a square wooden table in the dimly lit room, scooping cubes of tender beef with pieces of tangy, porous injera. John records us on the video camera we brought with us.

"Please say hello to our American friends," he requests of Berhanu and Girma.

"Hello," they say.

"What about me?" You can hear my voice, tiny and enthusiastic, beyond the view of the lens.

John turns the camera toward me. "Hello!" I say and wave, chewing and wiping my fingers. I am happy. We're almost there.

It is 6:30 a.m. in Adigrat. Girma takes us slowly along the rough, packed earth. The mountains in front of us have seen everything. Their outlines are so precise they seem like cutouts in the sky.

"The Savior of the World!" Berhanu says as we pull up to the Medhani Alen Catholic Church with its blond dome, red doors, and statue of Jesus with one arm raised high. We stop at a market for water and bread. Along the way, we pick up a distant cousin of the girls'.

"This is the day the girls were born," the cousin tells us through Berhanu.

In the United States, Helen had told us that the girls had no official birthdate. She gave us a range of possible dates and suggested we select a day in January. The agency agreed. But apparently, no one had bothered to ask the girls' family.

I write the cousin's words down. I am certain that if I do not, in the future I will believe I must have dreamed them.

We drive slowly as the road thins and then disappears, as if it has surrendered to the commanding natural landscape around us. Helen had told us the road would end and we would have to walk for an hour to meet the girls and their family. Marjorie dismissed this information as another one of Helen's fantastic stories.

Girma pulls the car to a gentle stop among small bunches of beavertail cactus with stems as wide and flat as paddles and decorated with bristles like stubble on a man's face. There are only three yards between us, but the men's voices sound tinny and faraway. Underneath my feet, the earth is as light and packed as brown sugar. Within arm's reach is a small island of green bordered by a layer of rocks. In its center stands a tree with a thin trunk and a flowering crown, like a tall, skinny kid with an Afro. In the distance more trees, some dense and willowy, stand in a line on faded, cracked earth. The sky is thick with all the blue left in the world.

It was important to set out early in the morning. We are near the Danakil Depression, one of the hottest places on Earth, where summertime temperatures can rise higher than one hundred twenty-five degrees Fahrenheit. It is December and only seventy-five degrees at the moment, but a pressing question among our guides is, How much heat can the Americans take? Berhanu makes a joke about melting Americans, and I laugh a bold "Ha-ha!" up at the sky. I am certainly not one of those people. I'm from this place, somewhere and some time back there, after all. And anyway, I'm decked out in my hardiest gear: hiking boots, cargo pants, a white long-sleeved, button-down shirt, and a broad-brimmed hat.

I nearly trip on titanic pieces of shale; my boots catch in the valley of crevices between them. The sun quickly discovers the skin beneath my hair, hat, and the rest of my clothing. I feel its piercing impact in my joints and lungs. If we had been in the States, if we were anywhere else, I would have been preoccupied with how soon I could seek out a piece of shade under which to hide. But here, even as I stoop, stumble, and trudge my way forward, I begin to understand that beneath this piercing sun and breathtaking sky is exactly where I belong. Everything lies in front of me; nothing is behind. There is no shelter, nowhere to hide. This sun: it may be relentless but it is glorious, too, evaporating any doubt about the road ahead. I stand up straight. The heat is not something to shun, I decide, but only something else to carry.

As we approach a group of thatched huts topped with perfect cylinders of long grass, my heart beats so rapidly that I reflexively cover it with my hand. I smooth my shirt and adjust my hat. I hope I look like what the family wants for their twins. As we are greeted by the people to whom the girls belong, I imagine a woman being presented to a groom at the inauguration of an arranged marriage.

"Be prepared to be treated like royalty," Helen had written in an unusually helpful email. Indeed the girls' family has slaughtered a sheep in our honor. A large platter of the roasted sheep meat sits on a clay table; the loaf of bread we bought in Adigrat is placed on the side. Everyone gathers to eat, but after a few token bites, I sit back on a bench molded from the same clay as the table and walls of the wide, circular room. I try to arrange my features into an expression that communicates my appreciation for the food, my desire to enjoy it, and my inability to do so. I am not successful, it is clear from the quality of the murmurs. "Emily doesn't like it," Berhanu says and smiles sympathetically; I can tell he is trying to translate the disappointment I have caused. It is terrible to know that I am failing to demonstrate the boundless depth of the gratitude I feel for everyone in this room. A torrent of emotion clogs my throat. My palms sweat and tingle. I am rigid with anticipation, eager for the wonderful, terrible moment in which the girls will be placed in our arms. Beside me John eats heartily and drinks sheep's milk from a tin cup. I cannot say no when the milk is offered to me. I feel multiple pairs of interested eyes on me as I bring the cup to my mouth.

The twins' grandmother brings out the baby we will know as Isabella. She is wrapped in the same light-blue quilted outfit that she wears in a picture that Helen sent months ago. Her grandmother, a slight woman with a lightly wrinkled face, stands in a space that separates two rooms of the family home. The sky shines a movie-star light down on the two of them. Isabella regards me dispassionately as she takes in the entire scene.

Giulia emerges midwail. "She is afraid because she has never seen white skin," Berhanu says, and gently touches John's arm. Giulia continues to cry as we stand outside the compound and are presented with carrots so bright and large they could serve as props in a Bugs Bunny cartoon. John gathers us together for a photograph before we begin the trek back to the Land Rover.

The return hike feels more arduous, the sun hotter, the air drier. I am trying not to show my exhaustion. The grandmother has a swaddled Isabella strapped to her back. Her steps are light and efficient on veins of rock that protrude from the earth. I walk next to one of the babies' cousins, a girl of eleven or twelve. Her eyes are large and kind;

the braids in her hair shine. She wears Giulia, who seems to be dozing, on her back, underneath a cloth secured to her faded green dress. We take turns looking at each other, and then looking away before the other one catches us. There is so much I want to ask and tell her, but the membrane of language, fine and opaque at once, travels with us like a mobile glass partition. Even though it feels a bit silly, the next time I sense her looking, I meet her gaze and, for the second time today, put my hand over my heart. I press down hard. When she looks away, she is still smiling.

"You are a part of our family now," an older male cousin tells us, but that's it for good-byes. John and I are hustled into the car, whose rumbling engine inspires more caterwauling from Giulia. The babies are shuffled around. I hold Giulia, who screams and stares at me with tears cascading from her eyes. Isabella rests quietly in John's lap, snug in the nest of his arms and chest. Suddenly, she sits up and opens her mouth slightly. Sheep's milk spills out of her tiny body. Giulia follows suit. Before her second round, I take my hat and turn it upside down under her chin.

Three hours later, we have become almost used to the smell and the feeling of our daughters' vomit caked on our clothing. We are sticky with heat and sweat and bodily fluids by the time we arrive at the airport in Mekele. John leaves the girls with me while he rushes to the bathroom to clean out my hat and rinse Isabella's excretions from his shirt. With a baby tucked into the crook of each arm, I sink into a plastic chair. My dizziness and blurry vision must be a result of the heat, I think. An older woman wearing a black hijab sits down next to me. She holds her arms open.

I hand her Giulia, and she pulls a small blanket from her belongings and hands it to me. She and John each take one of my arms when it's time to board.

I still feel rickety as we walk toward the plane, but I have a firm grip on Isabella, who emerges from the cloth on my shoulder as slowly as a plant sprouting from the earth in a time-lapse video. She stretches her neck like a periscope and pivots her head slowly, a stern look on her face. Like a general assessing a battlefield, or Magellan surveying the Atlantic, I think, and when she smiles, I believe we are sharing our first private joke.

Giulia has decided that it is my particular job to tend to her, so John and I trade babies once we are seated. She and I fall asleep quickly after takeoff. A few minutes later, a wave of pain propels me out of my seat and toward the bathroom. Along the way, I shove a miserable, indignant Giulia into the arms of a pretty flight attendant. I am on my hands and knees, in the throes of thudding, seizing abdominal pain, when the attendant knocks on the door. As soon as I undo the latch, she snatches the door open. I look up. She is stony; I am perpendicular. "Madame, your baby," she sniffs, and presents me with Giulia, who looks down at me with what appears to be alarm on her twelve-month-old face.

The thing about unpasteurized milk is that it does not agree with everyone. I spend the next few days at various tight angles on and around the floor of our hotel bathroom, my stomach in a losing war against bacteria. Gradually, I am able to climb onto the bed at night, where I lie on my back, breathing deeply, mouth open. Late at night, John takes the girls to the lobby when they become restless. Once, Giulia dozes while John calms Isabella by pushing her two inches back and forth until the short, rhythmic motion coaxes her to sleep.

Our flight back to the United States leaves in four days. We had planned to stay in Addis another week, but we moved up the date of our return after Marjorie and Yonas assured us that the finalization of the adoption would be simple and straightforward. The girls spend much of their time in the foster home, which is a requirement for the adoption process. Once I am well again, I feel only slightly guilty for enjoying these days of freedom from nascent motherhood. There is so much to see, even in the hotel lobby. On his late-night trips, John becomes friendly with Abeba, a beautiful young woman with a blossom of curly hair who manages one of the kiosks. When I meet her, she is standing next to a glass case that holds gold watches, stainless-steel cigarette lighters, and pendants shaped like Coptic crosses. Soon she will open her own clothing and jewelry shop. She asks about the twins and nods when I tell her they are spending the day at the foster home.

In the business center, I update friends and family via email, and try to ignore what is going on in front of me: an American with a face the color of marbled ham hisses at a hotel employee. She turns and smiles wanly. "Yes, sir?" I describe the interaction to Loree in an email. "I am so tired of this dynamic," I write. I have already described the scene at the bar: white men in business suits and military gear, loud and bloated with alcohol or power or both, pulling laughing brown women by the arm and letting their fleshy hands travel down the women's backs. Abeba tells me that some of the women are prostitutes and such scenes are common at large hotels in the capital.

The soldiers are here because Ethiopia has entered another phase of its epic war with Somalia. "Ethiopia just dropped a bomb," I report to friends. But it is terrifying to walk through the lobby past white men in camouflage and black berets. I have never seen so many guns in one place and up close. Soldiers stroll the hallways, holding high-powered rifles and guns against their bodies as they peer through the glass of the kiosks.

John and I spend most mornings at an Italian café just outside of the hotel and watch the world go by. We hear Arabic, Italian, and French. We meet an Australian journalist and his Ugandan girlfriend. We befriend a couple from Ireland. The woman pushes a sleeping brown baby in a stroller; the father holds the hand of a small brown girl in a pink dress and fancy shoes. John takes pictures of them and other people that we meet, but the subjects of most of his photographs are what we eat and drink: crunchy biscotti packed with almonds; fresh cannoli bursting with sweet ricotta; short, shapely bottles of Pellegrino; and espresso served in small, gleaming silver cups. He also takes photos of what we don't eat, like thick columns of salami and prosciutto in the market adjacent to the pasticceria.

These are moments of peace that we steal before plunging into the chaos that now determines the course of our days, which turn into weeks of frantic activity and confusion. We turn in circles in Addis, spinning like bumper cars from one bureaucratic holdup to another. The names on the girls' birth certificates are in the wrong order; this mistake costs us a day at the immigration office. Incorrect information on their passports takes almost a week to fix. Other key documents are botched. We go again and again to the U.S. embassy, only to be turned away each time. My heart sags when Yonas confesses the depth of his inexperience, but we are still sure it will work out in the end. He has successfully completed the adoption for another American couple, a considerate and scrupulous pair from Montana, whom, like us, he had inherited from Helen.

Helen has found us. We have not seen her, but she calls our hotel room at odd hours. Sometimes the phone rings just as we enter our room. I feel surrounded. She is not the person I once tried to enchant under a pavilion in Vermont. This woman is ugly with fury and wild with rage at the agents and the world in which they, along with every other human being, live. *No one* appreciates her talent and industry. *Everyone* is trying to "ruin" her; she is the target of a conspiracy and a victim of slander. Then she changes course and begins whimpering about her knee, which she has hurt recently.

"I'm sorry," I say.

I would happily break Helen's knee myself if it would render her unable to visit our hotel and skulk around the lobby, waiting for us to appear. She has thoroughly alienated the couple from Montana, whose soon-to-be son is a two-year-old named David. One day John and I sit with them in the hotel lobby as Helen approaches us, arms outstretched. The new parents pull David close and walk away. John chokes back his own rage, but I greet Helen warmly. It is the Scheherazade legend in reverse: I must pay attention to the narrative she is weaving in order to save my life.

Helen tells us the bureaucratic struggles we have been having are actually the result of nefarious activity on the part of the agency, that den of thieves. "Don't tell Yonas any of this," she warns.

I tell Yonas all of this the next morning when he comes to take us to the foster home. As much regret as I feel for having occasioned the anguish on his face, his distress upon hearing Helen's story reassures me. At least he is the person he has seemed to be all along.

We take the twins with us to the embassy this time, hoping that the sight of the girls will elicit some sympathy for our predicament. An agent with thick brown hair parted on the side calls us to her window. Her hands appear to be shaking as she points out yet more inaccuracies in our papers. She looks at me and Giulia, who rests in my arms.

"Have you been working with Helen Franklin?" she asks.

"Yes," I say.

"This case has to be reinvestigated."

I scramble to disown Helen, but it's too late. The agent informs us that reinvestigations sometimes take months.

"Please be honest. Is it possible that the girls may never be ours?"

"Yes," she says. Her voice is soft.

The tears are uncontrollable. I look down at Giulia. I will always remember you, I think, but you will never remember me. She gives me a look, like *Lady, lighten up*.

A week later, the same agent calls to congratulate us: we are parents and free to return to the States with our new daughters. She does not mention Helen, and we do not ask.

Helen never calls us again, and we never call her. But when she sends me a friend request on Facebook, I accept without telling John. Despite the pain and terror she has occasioned in my life, when I see her profile picture, I feel gratitude.

Before we leave, John, Giulia, Isabella, and I have breakfast in the hotel restaurant with Marjorie and Linda, another representative from our American agency, who happen to be in Addis on business. One of them complains about the "weird" food in the country. "Thank God for good old bacon and eggs!" she says, and I wish I could stand with a banner that says, THIS WOMAN DOES NOT BELONG TO US.

Marjorie and Linda have Helen stories to tell, but I am weary and happy and don't care anymore. I recall the visit we made yesterday to the foster home. Giulia was asleep on a couch with a dried stream of milk drool stuck to one side of her mouth. Even this sweet image is powerless against the nasty chatter, however, so I try to imitate John's look of honest concern.

A group of black Americans sits at a neighboring table. I am excited, having encountered no other black people from the States thus far. They wear matching T-shirts that read "Black to Africa Tour." I smile at them as I walk to the breakfast bar. I hear two women among them talk loudly about "white people who come here and steal our children."

They can't mean me, I protest internally as I take a plate and survey the food under the heated lamps. I am black like them, after all. Aren't I exempt? I look around the room for offending white couples and see our Irish friends and their children in the lobby outside the restaurant. I ladle eggs onto my plate. Though we are all parents of black children, I think, we are not the same.

But this isn't true. I know it isn't true because the thought stays trapped in my mind and fails to travel south to my gut, that place of deep bodily knowing. I am nothing like the Black to Africans. Instead I am just like our new Irish friends, along with other grinning new parents—white parents—in this hotel who tote brown children in BabyBjörns fastened to their backs and fronts. If they are thieves, then I, too, am a thief. I am not sorry.

Before we leave, we spend a lot of time with Eleazar, who reprises his role as shepherd. He takes us to the Zebra Café, where we meet his friend Kelile, who speaks English and adores Ernest Hemingway. The same day he escorts us to the home of another friend, a young woman named Fana, who hosts a coffee ceremony for all of us. As is the tradition, she roasts green coffee beans over hot coals, and then waves the smoke in our direction so that we can savor the aroma before she crushes the beans with a mortar and pestle. Along with coffee, she serves us khat, a leafy green plant with amphetamine-like properties. We chew the leaves and wait for the high. No luck. Fana and I share no common language, but we giggle like kids and trade accessories—her scarf for my glasses—for the duration of the ceremony.

We meet Aster again, too. She introduces us to her twin sister who, though not identical, looks like her exactly. They give us a tour of their factory, where men and women sit at rows of looms moving their hands in tandem as precisely as harpsichordists.

We spend a lot of time with the kids at the foster home, all boys, and all eager to show us packets of pictures from their American families-to-be. When we enter the building, they scream, "Yes!" but mostly for John, who makes a percussion instrument out of his body so that the boys can perfect the hip-hop dance moves they saw on the foster home television before Helen took it away out of spite.

There are also people we don't meet whom I will never forget, like the comely young Italian couple I pretended not to watch in the Zebra Café as they argued loudly and gorgeously, the woman's shiny black hair swinging like a blade, and their equally stunning brown baby howling in a high chair between them, as if staking his claim in the disagreement between his new parents.

I see the Italian couple again in line at the Addis airport ticket counter along with other fellow parents or bandits or both. The languages and accents of Italy, England, the Netherlands, and America fix us new parents as securely as pins on a map. Everywhere I turn, brown children are crying and still; peaceful and fussy; blank-eyed and staring. Soon they will jet off to disparate corridors of the world and experience never-before-imagined adventures in cities, towns, and villages that have not yet imagined them. Perhaps they will make whole lives where they land, or maybe curiosity and circumstance will keep them forever in motion.

. . .

We have two hours to kill before our flight boards, so I wheel a napping Isabella around the airport terminal. In the window of a clothing kiosk I see a dress. It is a simple *habesha kemis,* which is marketed in the States as an Ethiopian coffee dress due to its ubiquity at coffee ceremonies. A long, embroidered, dark green Coptic cross, bordered in black, decorates the front. Green and black lattice stitches outline the neck, hem, and sides of the dress, which is a long, fluid rectangle with short, wide sleeves. As I hold the dress against my body, the shopkeeper smiles in greeting and then continues her conversation with another woman in rapid Amharic. They lean into each other from opposite sides of the counter, their words a series of high, tender clicks. Each woman has big liquid eyes that look as if they have been outlined in kohl, a cosmetic as ancient as the Bronze Age but banned for years in the States because of its lead content. They keep their bodies close while they observe Isabella in her stroller, her head lolling to the side. The woman behind the counter asks me a question in Amharic.

"I'm sorry," I say.

"Oh, you're American!" exclaims the shopkeeper and puts her hands together.

I nod, pleased to be taken for a native, one of them, in the final hours of this journey.

"Your daughter?" The friend gestures at Isabella.

"Yes. She was born here. In Adigrat."

The two women nod as their eyes move from me to Isabella.

"You're very *good,*" the shopkeeper concludes. She looks at me gravely and puts her hand over her heart.

"No, no," I respond. "I am *lucky*." I try to match my look to hers and, for the third time since I have been in Ethiopia, put my hand over my own heart. A current of understanding passes between us, and I feel a wave of relief.

I leave the store carrying the dress in my hand, and two lines from our exchange that rush like a waterfall through my entire being, assuaging forever the rage I felt toward Helen, and circulating inside of me like blood for many years to come: *Your daughter? Yes.*

Going Home

My brother Warren calls on Thanksgiving to tell me that my grandmother in Mississippi has passed away. Her health had been declining steadily for several years. A series of strokes left her weaker and weaker. Severe arthritis turned her strong, wide fingers gnarled and stiff. A foam collar helped the constant pain in her neck that made it difficult for her to hold up her head. The gout that had afflicted her for years made walking a chore. But when she felt well enough, and the weather was particularly nice, she went outside to wander slowly through her garden, where she grew peas, cucumbers, tomatoes, and lettuce.

I step into the mudroom in order to talk to Warren, from whom I also learned of my mother's death on the morning of Christmas Eve five years ago. "Remind me never to take a call from you on a holiday again," I say to him. We laugh grimly and then make plans to meet in Mississippi in January. Actually, we make plans to make plans. Both of us are occupied today. Our brother James and his family, and my sister-in-law Joan and her family, have come to Burlington to spend the holiday with us. This is the first Thanksgiving that John and I are hosting, and we have been immersed in planning the menu and prettying the house for weeks. I say good-bye to Warren and bend to pick up my daughters' stray gloves and hats.

Laughter and busy conversation drift in from the table in the other room.

It's not right. It's not right to hear from my brother in New York about my grandmother's death in Mississippi while I am in Vermont. We have already had our first snowfall. It is currently eighty degrees in Mississippi. It isn't natural, but here we are. I share the news of my grandmother's death with the rest of my family. James and I accept condolences and say things like "It was her time" and "She lived a good, long life." Before we eat, we bow our heads and count our blessings. My grandmother was ninety-four years old.

On the morning of my trip to Mississippi, the line at the US Airways counter bulges left and right and snakes back toward the shop where you can purchase Vermont sweatshirts, maple syrup, and chocolates. I have already bought Vermont gifts for my aunts and cousins. I stand at the back of the line, trying to pull my body and bags as close as possible. A white woman behind me exclaims, "Lord, have mercy!" She has left her watch behind. Suddenly, I can feel her breath on my neck. "Have you got the time?" she asks. I turn the face of my watch toward her. She likes my watch; she likes my bag; it's so cold here; am I from Vermont?

I turn around. Thank you; it *is* cold; no, but I've lived here for thirteen years; I'm actually from the South.

She is from North Carolina. I suspected she was from the South the minute she leaned in so close to me. A black friend from Boston, a singer, once toured through the South with his musical ensemble. Southerners had no respect for other people's personal space, he reported upon his return. This regional characteristic must be a consequence of the geographical advantages the South had over the North, he speculated. In other words, because southerners had so much physical space, they did not have to carve out imaginary space in public places by hiding behind newspapers on the T, for instance, as he typically did.

The woman from the South chats happily about what a good time she has had in Vermont. She wears bright gold chains around her neck, neat black pants, and shiny loafers. Her fingernails are painted tomato red. There are bronze highlights in her hair and a thin layer of makeup on her face. Her pink sweatshirt I recognize as the same style as those available in the gift shop behind us. It is as if she has tried to dress casually in order to fit in with the laidback style of Vermont, but her accents have betrayed her. I think about the monochrome black color of my clothing, my fingernails raw and bitten to the quick. My South is black, but I will stand out there as dramatically as I stand out in Vermont.

The line through security moves slowly. Ahead of me, I see a black man wearing a sweatshirt with "Tennessee" emblazoned on the front, a pronouncement of his otherness as frank as his dark skin. We smile at each other the way black people do when we are surrounded by white people. The smile says, *You are here, and I am, too,* and *Isn't it interesting the way things turn out?*

My connecting flight to Jackson is delayed. I have five hours to roam Washington-Reagan International Airport. The delay is a gift. I am free, accountable to no one in this building. I find a Starbucks and then drift to an empty gate with no posted flights, as if the workday here has yet to begin. Like hotel rooms, airports are blank slates, settings in which it is possible to put aside real life, at least for a while. I unload my computer bag and rub my sore shoulder. I sit down, caress my coffee cup, and watch the people passing by, imagining the stories they carry. Anything is possible.

A small group has gathered underneath a television monitor near me. There has been a shooting in Maryland. Two people are dead, including the shooter, Darion Aguilar. He was sweet and gentle, says Aguilar's mother. He had an obsession with Columbine and dressed to resemble those shooters. I stand and join the small crowd in front of the monitor. Judging from his face, hair, and name, I presume that Aguilar is Latino, or black, or both. "He had to be black," my mother would say, and shake her head, whenever she read or watched a news report about a black man who had committed a crime, as if the blackness of the criminal was itself a crime against the race as a whole. I brace myself and wait for some mention of Aguilar's race but there is none.

A commercial comes on and the group breaks apart. As they turn in my direction, I can read the people from the way they are dressed: white airline personnel, black men in maintenance uniforms, and travelers of all races. A white businessman with his suit jacket hooked over his shoulder saunters past me toward the window. The cardboard circle around my coffee cup drops to the floor at the same time as a black man pushes a broom near my row. He picks up the cardboard strip and holds it toward me. We smile at each other. Everywhere around me are black

men: travelers and workers, manning kiosks and comput-
ers, reeling off flight information into microphones. The
farther south I get, the more black men I see. The more
black men I see, the safer I feel.

Not every black person here is black in the same way.
The woman with sleek dark braids selling electronics at
a nearby kiosk tells me she is from Ethiopia. Brazenly, I
insist on a secondary kinship by showing her pictures of
my daughters, who were born in her country. As soon as
she is able to finish her studies, she tells me, she will return
to Ethiopia. Standing and sitting next to kiosks up and
down the hall of this terminal are brown men and women
with accents from African countries and the Caribbean.
Some of them are here to stay but work extra jobs in order
to send money to families back home. Others plan to make
their way back someday. All of them are in between, here
now but always elsewhere.

A black woman with short natural hair and gold,
wire-rimmed glasses scans tickets into a machine as my
flight boards. A balding white man in a business suit and
I approach her at the same time. I step quickly in front
of him and my heart races. The semester has recently
started, and my students and I have just completed the
Narrative of the Life of Frederick Douglass. For the last few
hours of my layover, I have been reading *Incidents in the
Life of a Slave Girl* by Harriet Jacobs. In this moment, I
am acutely aware that, in the not-so-distant past, relatively
speaking, relative to the history of the human race, that
is, a black woman stepping in front of a white man would
have been a consequential act. So much of the history
of black and white, I think, is contained in the arrangement of our bodies. Probably the white man is not think-

ing these thoughts. But maybe he, too, is considering my act as one with historical significance. Maybe he, like me, marvels at the transformation in the choreography of race relations, and how remarkable it is, the way things have turned out.

My phone buzzes as soon as we land.

Where are you?! reads Warren's text. He arrived in Hazlehurst early in the afternoon.

In Jackson, I punch into the tiny keyboard. *I'm starving. Should I eat?*

NO.

But I can't wait. I stuff the fast-food wrappers into the glove compartment of my rental car and drive south to Hazlehurst. Along the way, I worry about my family in Burlington, my students. Have I left enough work for them to do in my absence? I know they are grateful for the two days of freedom. I roll down my window and take in the cool Jackson air. I am free, I think for the second time today. If I wanted to, if I had to, I could disappear into this city where no one knows me. I could begin again.

Driving while daydreaming always ends the same way for me. *I'm lost,* I text my brother after pulling into the parking lot of the Piggly Wiggly. I have been circling the same landmarks: Walmart, the Holiday Inn Express, the Sonic drive-in, and this grocery store. I thought I would be able to feel my way to my grandmother's house; I thought the map of Hazlehurst was stenciled inside of me. I was wrong. Aunt Julia comes to find me in my aunt Ann's

Chevy Tahoe. When she rolls down the window, my breath catches: her face is my mother's face. I follow her home, flush with both sorrow and joy.

Aunt Ann and my cousins are waiting at my grandmother's house. When we arrive, I distribute the presents I bought in Vermont. It's after midnight and everybody is exhausted, weary from travel and waiting and eating from the feast on the table that Aunt Julia had prepared in anticipation of our visit. As I pile fried chicken, yams coated with roasted marshmallows, and black-eyed peas cooked with ham hocks onto my plate, I think guiltily of the fast-food wrappers. I eat and sit and talk with my family and make plans to eat and sit and talk with them again tomorrow.

My brother James calls to say hello and ask about sleeping arrangements. He's curious in particular to find out who will be sleeping in the bed in which my grandmother died. It was going to be me, but now that James has brought it up, I feel a little weird about it. Warren offers to trade rooms.

Soon I am lying on a bed with a wrought-iron frame in a room that my mother's three sisters once shared. I lie on my back with my arms folded behind my head as soft laughter emanates from the living room. I am warm and safe in a sturdy old house in this faraway place with people whom I love and who love me back. I have just fallen asleep when I hear the song of a summer bird, a robin or a blue jay. The sound is as improbable as it is gentle and pure. I drift back to sleep, and the bird's song borders my dream like a piece of thin, delicate lace.

. . .

Neither Warren nor Aunt Julia heard the bird last night, I discover in the morning. They are already sitting at the table eating breakfast by the time I emerge. The sky is slightly overcast, but the sun's bright judgment pierces through the curtains anyway, insisting that we begin the day. It's time to pay a visit to my grandmother.

A homegoing is an African American Christian funeral service. Like *passing* or *crossing over,* the term *going home* is a euphemism for death. The roots of the homegoing tradition date back to the Atlantic slave trade, and reflect a belief that one's pure African soul would return to the motherland upon death, where it belonged.

I read about homegoings in a book. My grandmother couldn't have cared less about Africa, or homegoings, and wasn't interested in having any memorial service at all. She had outlived so many friends and relatives, she said, that she didn't think a service would be worthwhile. She asked that her body be taken directly from the funeral home to be buried in her family's plot behind her church. Her pastor wanted to hold a service anyway, but her children forbade it.

Warren, Aunt Julia, and I drive to the church to have a look at the gravesite. As we walk the rocky, uneven path to the family plot behind the church, I think about the services I attended nearly thirty years ago when I spent a summer in Hazlehurst with my grandmother.

Ostensibly, I was in Hazlehurst that summer in order to conduct a research project on the history of my family. It was not an easy summer. My grandmother and I argued.

One of the things we argued about was my approach to the project. The distant, anthropological lens I had adopted made her wary. She was suspicious. Why was I so eager to go to church, for instance, when so many people my age did everything they could to avoid it? Mostly, I wanted to go because I was bored. Also, the excitement of an authentic Southern Baptist church service, I thought, would enrich my work. It would be another story to take with me when I left, a story that I could bring to New Haven that would impress my friends and the summer research coordinator.

As much as she disapproved of how I was going about my work, my grandmother was also proud of me, and pleased to introduce me to her church community. I followed her into the small brick building and matched her pace as she worked her way down a line of men and women, shaking hands and extending personalized greetings. "You look as sharp as a rat's tail on a frosty morning," she said to one man in a maroon shirt and black suit. "All right, all right, now," he said as he took her arm at the elbow and shook her hand. Smiling faces beamed in her direction, everyone hoping for the blessing of her wit. *All right, all right.* My grandmother, known as Miss Dotsie, moved easily from one person to the next, less walking than gently rocking down the line. Most of the time I spent with her that summer was in her house, where the world came to her. Here she was, out in the world, and it was ready for her. It had been waiting.

The service began with an organ and a prayer. The choir, whose members were outfitted in long red robes, began the first song, "Have You Got Good Religion?"

Have you got good religion?
Certainly Lord
Have you got good religion?
Certainly Lord

Once the mood was set, the preacher began his sermon. He spoke about faith, forgiveness, and the power of redemption. His message was unremarkable, even predictable, I thought. But then his voice changed. First, he added a little vibrato. Then, a steady cadence emerged and held firm. Finally, his voice took flight.

"I *felt* something," I wrote in my journal that night. I sat mesmerized, listening as the preacher balanced his words precisely in a sacred space between speech and song. He maintained that balance and opened the door wide to the new space he had made. The choir entered, took up his rhythm, expanded it, glorified it, and then the organ joined them. The church was ablaze with something big, something bigger than language, something I had never experienced before. A few women jumped, shouted, and fell to the floor. Ushers were at the ready to assist the fallen. "I wanted to jump up, wave my hands," I wrote. But the staid traditions of the Episcopal Church in which I grew up held me back. The church was now in a frenzy, the parishioners, pastor, choir, and ushers colliding and cohering, expanding and contracting, one hydra-headed organism. A thin woman in a pink suit and white tights appeared to faint. An usher knelt beside her and cupped her head in one hand, waving a fan with the other.

"I want so much to be a part of something like that. But I probably will never be," I wrote. "I was born to be a

spectator, to watch and feel but to keep my mouth closed."
The only release I could manage was to cry. I let the tears
fall, overwhelmed by the show of organic, spontaneous
vitality in the room, and awash in self-pity at my utter
aloneness. So, *this* was real life, I thought, from which I
was doomed to stand forever apart. My grandmother
glanced at me out of the corner of her eye.

That night I sang the songs I had heard in church
softly to myself as I was getting ready for bed.

> *Soon and very soon*
> *We are going to see the King.*
> *Hallelujah*
> *Hallelujah*
> *We're going to see the King.*

Even though the words were coming out in the Yankee
accent I had been refining since childhood, in my head, I
heard the glorious southern cadence of those robed men
and women. I whispered the lyrics and hugged the memory of the wild carpet ride I had taken with them that
morning. I felt happy and guilty, as if I had stolen something precious and no one would ever know.

We went to church again the next week. I tried to walk
like an ordinary person up to our pew, but I wasn't an ordinary person anymore. I had been a witness to a miracle;
I had experienced a true revelation. Nothing about me
would ever be the same again.

My excitement wilted as the service began and
unfolded exactly as it had the previous week. The preacher
spoke, then shook his words with vibrato, which cued the

chorus, who matched his gait, which signaled the organist, who added dimension, which stirred the people, some of whom shook loose and dropped to the floor.

What I had witnessed the week before was less an organism than an elegant machine; not chaos but perfectly crafted choreography. But fascination quickly elbowed disappointment off the stage of my imagination. This was real life—no magic, only practice, commitment, and labor. This lesson, about life, about art, is one I am still learning.

We say good-bye to my grandmother and the relatives buried alongside her and decide to take a walk around the town square. Hazlehurst is the county seat of Copiah County. It is a city, but it feels like a small town, with a population of fewer than four thousand people, 70 percent of whom are African American. Despite its percentage of black citizens, like most cities in America, the majority of the people in positions of power in Hazlehurst are white. Mississippi was once known as the lynching capital of the South, but no one I have talked to here has any stories about that degree of violence between black and white. There is evidence of progress. Blues musician Robert Johnson is touted as an official native son. A plaque that details his achievements is posted next to the train depot. Still, old attitudes endure. The day after the 2008 presidential election, there was no mention in the local newspaper of the victory of President Obama. There was only an editorial reflection on the effects of the campaign season. "Life-long friends became bitter enemies," wrote Joe Buck Coates. "Workplaces are divided and workers become suspicious of each other's intentions. Even some families are pulled apart because of ideological differences." Now that the dust has settled, advised Coates, the most important thing for readers to do was thank veterans for the freedom to vote at all.

The three of us walk slowly up and down the few streets that constitute the square, passing the post office, a place to cash checks, several law offices, and a clothing store for women. We pause to step into a shop full of antiques where, as toddlers, my daughters Giulia and Isabella admired two glass figurines shaped like ducks. I remember how they pushed the pads of their thumbs against the pointy orange beaks over and over. Behind us is a bridge whose steep arc makes it impossible to see over to the other side. I love this bridge and this particular street, whose abundance of empty storefronts reminds me of a deserted movie set for an old Western that I saw once at Universal Studios. I see Bologna, too, a city in Italy that my husband John and I visited years ago, in the rubbed, faded colors of the buildings' facades. I love this place for the freedom it gives me to remember, and invent.

This South is nothing like the South in which I used to live, with its manicured lawns and gated country clubs. Even that South has changed. Over the years, Nashville has gotten bigger and more complex. The relatively modest, adolescent city in which I was born has grown into an adult with a tailored suit and gym-toned thighs, all glamour and muscle. It is part of the New South. In that South, there is no place for my daydreams. My true South, this South, is old, and deep, well into the belly of the region, far below the Mason-Dixon Line.

My mother never wanted to spend her life in either the Old South of Mississippi or the New South of Nashville, but that's how things turned out. Returning to Hazlehurst was never an option, but she is here, in the faces and memories of my aunts, cousins, and other family members who never left. Here she is not Harold's wife, or even my mother. She is Clara Jean, or Moochie, a childhood nickname that she loathed, and which I am free to divulge here because she is no longer alive to stop me. I don't know where Moochie comes from or what it means, and my aunts were too young at the time of her rechristening to remember.

I have always been greedy for stories about my mother's family, even before she died and I became overwhelmed with the continuous sensation of being unmoored. For many years, I believed that in these stories were clues to who I was, and who I would become. This is why I decided to spend the summer of my junior year in college in Hazlehurst, and it is, ultimately, why I am here now.

Aunt Julia, Warren, and I pass Town Hall and the library where, thirty years ago, I spent hours looking through old newspapers, census reports, and wills, trying to find evidence of the interracial love affair that began the Jefferson family line. My cousin dropped me off most of the time, but sometimes I would borrow my grandmother's brown Chevy and drive right by Town Hall into downtown Hazlehurst, where I would park, walk around, and agonize over my research. My grandmother was not happy that I was looking into that old story. She worried that my project would cause trouble, that it would somehow become public and resurrect old wounds, possibly even upset race relations in town. She took me to visit family landmarks reluctantly, uneasy about my desire to take photographs and explore on foot. "You get to leave, but I have to live here," she would remind me.

I felt my grandmother's eyes on me constantly. Privacy was hard to come by, so I would stay in my bedroom well into the morning. I could hear my grandmother speculating to friends and relatives who stopped by about how I would spend my day while I pretended to be asleep. My journal entries from that summer are full of longing and confusion. Here were people that I looked like and felt like, but that I was nothing like at the same time. "How did it happen?" I wrote. "They are my family." I hated that my voice was so different from theirs, that my speech faltered when I was around them. I felt pinched and small and foreign. My grandmother sat on the porch and held court while I stayed inside and read. *Anna Karenina* helped me escape; the stories of Alice Walker offered a way in. But I could not enter; I could not find my way across the threshold. I wrote letters to friends up north in which I transformed Hazlehurst into Faulkner's Yoknapatawpha County and portrayed its citizens as the kinds of oddball characters one might find in a Eudora Welty novel. I did not write of my awkwardness and inability to connect with people with whom I shared the same genes and moods and history.

The tension between my grandmother and me erupted into a fight about Jesse Jackson. Neither my grandmother nor I was very interested in politics, but during the summer of 1988, Jackson was in the middle of his second presidential campaign. The promise and excitement of Jackson's message moved me. It was a reprieve from the still, hot days spent under my grandmother's watchful eye. My wild idealism butted heads with my grandmother's pessimism. She didn't care for Jackson, and she didn't care for his civil rights background. Like some other black southerners of her generation, she saw civil rights activists as outside agitators who did more harm than good to southern race relations. She had no love for the Democratic Party in general, and blamed President Carter for the cuts in her Social Security check. Her words surprised me. In my comfortable, middle-class Nashville home, Jimmy Carter was spoken of with reverence. "He was too decent for the presidency," my parents would say and shake their heads. My mother expressed the same grim sympathy for Carter as she did for the black men on television in handcuffs who, it would turn out, had been punished for crimes they didn't commit. "They were always out to get him," she said. And I knew the *they* that hated Jimmy Carter was the same *they* that hated black people, hated us.

My grandmother and I brokered a peace based upon an unspoken mutual feeling of pity. She thought I was naïve and foolish. I saw her attitudes as sad vestiges of the past. But I didn't know anything about her particular past. I didn't know, for instance, that among the civil rights activists who came to organize the citizens of Hazlehurst *were* outside agitators who wreaked havoc on her community. Today, Aunt Julia describes to me how a cadre of activists from points north landed in Hazlehurst like a tornado and shook the black world at its foundation. A central player in the drama was Rudy Shields, she says, an activist of national renown who traveled from Chicago to Mississippi in 1965 to organize strikes and boycotts. My grandfather offered to help. He had friends among whites in the community and he knew how they felt about black people. He understood the way Hazlehurst worked from the perspective of both blacks and whites, and he suggested tactics that were appropriate to the distinct culture of the place. Shields and his group ignored him.

My grandfather, like others of his clan, like me, was proud, impulsive, quick to anger, and easy to offend. He crossed picket lines and forced his embarrassed daughters to attend boycotted schools. But his acts of rebellion notwithstanding, the black community of Hazlehurst was broken. In 1965 Hazlehurst had about thirty-four hundred residents. When the movement touched down, it was literally neighbor against neighbor, my aunt tells me. Black people shot bullets into the homes of other black people who were seen as antagonistic to the cause. Perhaps because of my grandfather's contrariness, perhaps as a consequence of the envy the family elicited in the community, the Jeffersons proved handy targets. My grandfather was threatened with physical violence. He heard of a plan afoot to cut off his youngest daughters' long hair. My grandfather spent many nights sitting in a rocking chair in his living room with the lights off, a rifle balanced on his lap. My grandmother carried a small hatchet in her purse whenever she took her usual shortcut through the fields that separated her from her parents.

My aunt tells this story as we drive slowly around Hazlehurst. She points out the houses of former family enemies whose descendants she now considers friendly acquaintances. We drive up and down Extension Street, with its parade of regal, antebellum homes and languid, aristocratic willow trees decorating the front yard. Two blocks later, we pass carcasses of abandoned houses, each one held together weakly by rotting wood. The windows look as if they have been punched, shards of glass hanging from their frames, like rows of mouths with broken teeth. In this neighborhood my grandmother's parents used to live.

I ask Aunt Julia about present-day class dynamics in town, the differences between the lives of the rich and the poor. Where do we fit in this picture? I ask her. She thinks for a moment. "Well, I guess we're poor," she says. Her answer startles us both.

When I was a child, and the roads around my grandmother's home were made of dirt and loose gravel, her house was easily the nicest on the block. It was certainly the proudest, distinguished by its story of origin. The house is my grandmother's grandest achievement, her dream inscribed in its foundation like initials etched in concrete.

My grandmother was born in Hazlehurst in 1919. My mother, her oldest child, was born in 1938. My grandmother never admitted that she was forced to marry because of the pregnancy, Aunt Julia says, but it was clear that the pregnancy was an accident. She and my grandfather married quickly and quietly, sneaking off to the local justice of the peace.

When he was a young man, Julius Jefferson had a reputation. He came from a brood of handsome wastrels. He and his brothers had light skin and money. They were tall, charming, and lazy. Their father bought them a car and kept it filled with gas, even during the Depression. They drank, chased women, and never had to work. My grandfather's mother looked down on my grandmother and her family. "You better find somebody else to marry," she told my grandmother.

The Clausells, my grandmother's family, did not have money, but they were dignified and hardworking. Whenever I hear stories of my grandmother's parents, Mama Tempie and Papa Ran, I always imagine them as brownskinned versions of the couple in Grant Wood's 1930 painting *American Gothic*. Mama Tempie was not impressed by the relative wealth of the Jefferson clan. She disapproved of my grandfather and warned my grandmother not to take up with him. When my grandmother left my grandfather, very soon after their hasty wedding, she returned to Mama Tempie's house and discovered that her mother had discarded her clothes and burned all of the poetry that she had been writing since childhood.

Dotsie Clausell did not take up with Julius Jefferson because of his money or his looks. He was a way out. Julius, whom she called Jeff, had a brother with a job on the railroad in Texas. My grandfather was set to join him, and that's when he and Dotsie decided to get married. But Jeff's father decided to send another brother instead. Heartbroken, Dotsie abandoned the marriage and returned home to her parents, only to have her heart broken again when she found out what her mother had done to her precious belongings.

Dotsie was resourceful and industrious. She was determined to live a life bigger than what Hazlehurst could offer. With my mother, Clara Jean, who was then a toddler, in tow, she took a train to Chicago, where she had extended family. She didn't have money to rent an apartment of her own. Her relatives were short on space, so she lived with one set of cousins and put my mother in the care of another. The children in the family with whom my mother lived teased her cruelly. They were jealous of her straight hair and yanked off the ribbons that my grandmother had tied at the ends of her daughter's braids. Dotsie switched places with her daughter, but she couldn't find work that would enable her to buy independence for her and Clara Jean.

From Chicago, she traveled to Los Angeles, where she had other family, but again, she couldn't find suitable work. She knew field work and enjoyed physical labor, but there were no such opportunities. For a black woman there was always domestic work, but Dotsie knew her parents would be embarrassed if she took a job cleaning the houses of white people, and she could not bring herself to shame them again.

So, Dotsie came home. In Hazlehurst she found a job working in a factory where she spent her days making little wooden boxes for strawberries. The box factory was located near the railroad tracks. Every day, on her way to and from work, my grandmother crossed those tracks, perhaps wondering each time if there was still a chance for her to be free.

At the time, Dotsie and Clara Jean were living with Mama Tempie and Papa Ran, but the atmosphere in the house was uncomfortable. Dotsie's mother still disapproved of her, but she fawned over Clara Jean, whom Mama Tempie viewed as a delicate, innocent victim of the mess my grandmother had made of her life. Her mother's judgment weighed heavily enough, but even worse was the knowledge that she and her daughter were drains on her parents' meager resources. Dotsie decided to build a house.

Not long after she returned to Hazlehurst, Dotsie and Jeff reunited. It wasn't an entirely unpleasant decision for my grandmother, but she didn't have much choice. Her mother had applied the full force of her religious certitude, and reminded her daughter over and over that regardless of the legal status of her marriage, she and Jeff were still, and always would be, husband and wife in the eyes of God. And then Jeff wanted her back. He intimidated every man who showed any kind of romantic interest in his estranged wife. It was only in the factory, doing the repetitive work on the assembly line, laughing with and teasing her sister Bobbie, who worked alongside her, where Dotsie was free. Once she left that building, the strictures of her social world forced her down a single narrow corridor.

Jeff didn't want any part of Dotsie's plan to build a house. His family already owned a lot of property. Why go to the trouble and expense of building a house when they could live on his parents' land for free?

The idea of spending her life with her in-laws, who looked down on her family and had never accepted her—that was one sacrifice Dotsie was unwilling to make. She took on more shifts. She picked beans and collected discarded glass bottles, which she washed and resold to a store in town. Day after day, month after month, boxing and bending and washing, so many hot, long walks to and from town with bags of bottles in her arms, over her shoulder. Finally, she had earned nearly enough money for the materials. What she couldn't afford she got on credit from a lumber company, whose owners trusted her because of their friendship with Jeff. She had everything she needed, except her husband's permission to buy the land. No bank would give a woman a mortgage without a man's name attached.

After months of arguments and stony silence, Jeff relented. Dotsie hired her brother Frank and a family friend, known as Shot, to build her house. Shot and Frank used wood, sheetrock, and concrete, laboring day after hot, muggy, Mississippi day. The house they built had two bedrooms, a dining room, living room, bath, kitchen, and a screened-in porch. Shot and Frank made shutters and painted them white, like the house, according to Dotsie's instruction.

My mother was fourteen years old when the house was completed. Aunt Julia was only three, but she remembers how Clara Jean would stand in the front yard with her hands on her hips, smiling at the house that her mother, uncle, and Shot had built.

It took a long time for my grandmother to give up on her dreams of leaving Hazlehurst. Many years later, several years before she died, after my Aunt Julia had moved back home from California to care for her, Miss Dotsie told her second-born daughter, who was named after her husband, Julius, "If I had known I would be here all my life, I would have built a better house."

. . .

Aunt Julia tells us family stories as we sit around the dining room table, picking at food left over from the banquet my aunt prepared for Warren and me yesterday. I pull crunchy pieces of skin off a drumstick until the tender meat is exposed, glistening and naked. Warren leaves tonight. He is in the Jackson airport waiting for his flight back to New York to board while I lie on my back in my aunt's childhood bed, imagining my grandmother's wide, strong hands picking beans and writing poems made of ash. I am awakened in the night by the crack of a gunshot. I fall back to sleep visualizing fireworks trailing worms of light in the sky.

When I wake up, I find Aunt Julia in the living room fretting over the weather. Snow is in the forecast. Newscasters make ominous predictions. I smile and imagine what is sure to be a light dusting that has the entire city of Hazlehurst in a panic. I sit with my aunt and try to distract her. Her worried face is framed by a bevy of lush green plants. "Even the plants have plants," I tell James when he calls again.

This is Aunt Julia's house now. When it sagged from termite damage, she replaced the worn carpet with smooth wood floors. She had the tiny, awkward kitchen ripped out and a new one put in. Surrounding trees sometimes dent the metal roof, which then leaks. But the roof will always be metal, because that was what her mother wanted. In a similar spirit, she maintains the two imposing cabinets of curios my grandmother treasured, and has added some knickknacks of her own.

Even more than these practical things, Aunt Julia's plants reveal her stake in the continuing vitality of her mother's house. Her plants are her progeny; she has no children. She cares for her brood of African violets, snake plants, ponytails, succulents, and Christmas cactuses as faithfully as she tends to the stories her mother bequeathed to her, and that she now entrusts to me.

The South of my aunt's childhood was mean. She remembers how her mother had to wait quietly for white customers to be served first in the neighborhood grocery store. She tells me about Wilson's on Highway 51, a meat store where black customers were once ignored as long as white customers were present.

I can't stand the image of my extraordinary grand-mother waiting humbly and silently to be recognized by white people. Miss Dotsie, who wrung the necks of chickens until they snapped, who cut off the heads of snakes with a garden hoe; this force of nature about whom tales both factual and apocryphal were spun, are still spun, standing and waiting simply to be seen. The deeper Aunt Julia gets into this story, the more layers she adds to her portrait of black life in the Jim Crow South, the more riled up we both become. We put on our jackets and head to Wilson's.

At first, Aunt Julia says she will stay in the car. But as it becomes clear to her that I am not only willing but eager to create a scene, she decides it would be best if she accompanied me. As a cover, she advises me to ask for a pound of cheddar cheese. I walk up and down the aisles slowly, casing the joint. My aunt's eyes meet mine across rows of crackers and canned goods. A little black girl, maybe ten years old, holding grape soda and a small bag of Funyuns, observes me seriously and then waves.

"May I have a pound of cheddar, please," I say, as I stand among the other customers, some black, some white. The pitch of my voice is the kind you might use when talking to a person with poor hearing against whom you are nursing a grudge. Behind the counter are white men and women wearing white coats and plastic gloves. The white man holding the cheese nods and cuts the block into precise, identical slices.

Oh, well. We wander out, take the cheese back home, and drive to Aunt Ann's house on Extension Street.

I come from a family of readers, so the afternoon plan is to go to Jackson, forty miles north, to visit the nearest bookstore. Before we leave, I browse the shelves of Aunt Ann's bulging bookcases: James Patterson, John Grisham, and Stephen King, her favorite author. Like her sisters, Ann has enough books to outfit a small lending library. But there is always room for more books. We make the trip to Books-A-Million in Ann's Tahoe. I sit in the back with my cousin and her two children while my aunt recounts the story of the Jefferson family during the era of civil rights. She remembers how her mother's brother Frank and his wife, Bea, both of whom she adored and calls the loves of her life, donned their own rifles in the war between the Jeffersons and the activists. Uncle Frank blocked the driveway while Aunt Bea fired a warning shot in the air at the home of the most hostile antagonist. That particular aggressor never bothered another Jefferson again.

In my story about my husband's first visit to Hazlehurst, John is received immediately and warmly into the bosom of my maternal line. Aunt Ann tells a different story.

"Tell Emily not to bring that white man to my house," she instructed my grandmother.

"Emily is your niece," my grandmother reminded her.

"Emily is welcome but he isn't."

Neither John nor I had any idea what was waiting for us when we pulled into Aunt Ann's driveway. When they heard the car, Ann's husband, daughter, and a family friend fled to their rooms. Aunt Ann looked out of the window and saw John and me in the driveway, laughing and talking. "You looked like best friends," she said.

I love this romantic tale, but since I am as difficult as anyone else in my clan, it is just as likely that John and I were arguing in her driveway. Either way, however, the story ends the same way.

John won her over with what he didn't do. "He didn't try to hug me or call me 'Auntie,'" she explains. He didn't impose a false intimacy. Unlike generations of white people in the South whom my ancestors had no choice but to endure, John did not presume that her body was his to touch. Instead he held out his hand for her to shake.

"Now I don't think of John as white. He's just family," she says.

What has happened in the world while my aunts, cousins, and I have been nosing around a bookstore, driving to and from Jackson, telling family tales? Aunt Julia and I turn on the news as soon as we get back to Hazlehurst.

Which of the world's bank of stories have made it to the screen? The usual reports of violence, despair, success and failure, winning and losing, and, in Hazlehurst at least, talk and talk of snow. My flight to Vermont leaves tomorrow.

It's not the snow as much as the ice, Aunt Julia informs me the next morning. I knew it had snowed as soon as I woke up; the room was dazzlingly bright with its reflection. My aunt and I stand on the porch and observe the transformation of our street, the houses and cars now sparkling and frozen. We scoot our feet along the stone path to my rental car, which is encased in a thick film of ice.

"We can scrape it off with a credit card," says my aunt.

"Aunt Julia, there aren't enough credit cards in all of Hazlehurst to get the ice off this car."

Instead I turn the heat all the way up and let the engine run until the leather seats are warm and the windshield is beaded with water. I suggest we drive downtown and have a look around. I take the roads leading to the town square inch by inch. My flight to Burlington has been canceled.

We are not the only ones in the town square, standing and taking pictures of this odd, breathtaking scene. Icicles hang from poplar trees; people slip along streets like nervous amateur skaters. Two cars have been abandoned at the bottom of the bridge. Aunt Julia and I watch as a green Mustang fights valiantly for purchase, sliding back and starting forward, again and again, like the little engine that could. After some practice, we are able to walk with confidence past the granite Confederate soldier standing guard in front of the courthouse. Enough excitement. We warm our hands on the dashboard vents and creep slowly toward home.

It was God's will, my father says when I call him that night to tell him about the canceled flight and our afternoon adventure.

Aunt Julia had believed she could move back to Hazlehurst and keep her life in California, too. But maintaining my grandmother's house and health while keeping up her San Jose condo proved impossible. The decision to narrow her life into this small place was hard, but easy, too. The pastor at my grandmother's church told Julia she was needed at home in Hazlehurst. That was all she needed to hear. She maintains her friendships in California via letters and the telephone, which rings as often as it did during the long-ago summer I spent with my grandmother.

Around the same time that Aunt Julia lost her mother, she lost her longtime love, Walter, who lived in Jamaica. He died of a sudden heart attack.

My grandmother was always skeptical of romantic love. In her experience, men were work; marriage was duty. Two more children, both girls, were produced by the union of Dotsie and Jeff after Aunt Julia was born. The couple lived unhappily together on and off between my grandfather's military tours, until he passed away at the age of sixty-one.

Once, Aunt Julia showed her mother a postcard she had received from Walter on which he described how much he missed her and how often he thought of her. My grandmother studied it and then handed it back to her daughter. "I guess I never really loved anyone," she said.

Aunt Julia loved my grandmother, even though and because she was difficult. She loved my grandfather, his hard nature notwithstanding. She loves the house that was built in spite and because of the mutual stubbornness of her parents. She loves the plants that surround her beautiful Jefferson face, and that flourish in the oxygen they all share, the fuel that turns the engine of her stories.

That night as I lie in bed, a song comes billowing out of the darkness, "Nightshift" by the Commodores:

> *You found another home*
> *I know you're not alone*

The singer's voice is vivid and tender. His pace is even and sure. I imagine a kind man, a black man, sitting on his porch on this winter night, compelled to sing this song of promise, of welcome. I close my eyes and let the song hold me, blend me into the night and this place, and feel the boundaries between here and there disappear, the song rubbing away the distance between then and now, like water eroding stone.

"Are you ever coming back?" a student jokes in an email the following morning, after I write to inform my class that my flight has been delayed yet again.

The second delay turns out to be brief, just a few hours, long enough for Aunt Julia and I to linger over coffee while we watch newscasters interview city residents about how they fared in the storm. In between the news segments, we talk. We continue to talk as I pack my rental car. My suitcase, relieved of its gifts, is much lighter on this side of the journey. When I get into the car, Aunt Julia puts out her hand to take the lone fast-food wrapper that I missed. She stands by the driver's window as I try to convince her to visit us in Vermont. I wish it were possible to collapse the space between us; Mississippi and Vermont feel like opposite ends of the world.

"Don't get lost," Aunt Julia teases as I start the engine. She stands at the gate as I pull away slowly and wave. It's time to face the road ahead, and make my way to points north.

People Like Me

"Home is longevity," Ellie says when I ask what the word means to her. Ellie and I grew up together in Nashville. During our high school years, we slipped each other notes every day in class and spent hours every night on the phone. On weekends, we practiced dance moves side by side in front of mirrors in the rec room of my house. Never, during those years, could I have conceived of a life in which she would not be a constant presence.

Ellie teaches high school in St. Louis, where she has lived for most of her adult life. I have lived in Vermont for seventeen years, since John and I arrived to assume faculty positions at the university. Seventeen years and I still do not call Vermont home. Maybe I never will.

It is impossible not to like Vermont in the same way that it is impossible to dislike nature itself. This state contains some of the most breathtaking vistas in this country. Yet when I sit by Lake Champlain, or next to one of the many pristine natural springs, I see myself superimposed upon the landscape, raised and slightly askew, like a sticker in an activity book my daughters enjoyed when they were younger.

It is impossible, also, not to be tempted to idealize Vermont as a state with social justice woven into the fabric of its history and culture. I called my parents to gloat when

Vermont came in first on the night of both elections that made Barack Obama president. I bragged when Bernie Sanders, then a congressman, called a meeting for people of color at a church in downtown Burlington purely to find out how we were faring. As of this writing, Vermont is one of the few states in which no black man has been killed during a traffic stop. I cherish these details and list them for people who ask me what it is like to live black in such a white place. But Vermont, like any place, is complicated. Perhaps the reason why no black men have been killed by police during traffic stops is because there are few black men here in the first place.

Can I make a home here? Every day for the last seventeen years, the question has tagged along with me. My daughters' bus driver and I trade book recommendations in the morning as the girls clomp up the stairs to their seats: *Stay.* In the parking lot of the grocery store, a white man with a slick bald head looks at me, at my license plate, and then shakes his head in disgust: *Leave.* A thrilling early winter snowfall: *Stay.* A long, bitter spring of stomping through the slushy, dingy remains of that same snowfall and its successors: *Leave.* The tallying is continuous and exhausting. It is less a thought than a sensation. I hear it like the ticking of an old-fashioned scoreboard. *Stay. Leave.* Tick. Tick.

One April afternoon, I stomp through the snow and slush on a walk from campus to the public library downtown. "Ethiopian Boogie Benefit," a poster on a bulletin board announces. The event will take place in June in Lincoln, Vermont. The poster, decorated in red, yellow, and green, stands out among its neighbors: plain paper advertisements for yoga classes, book groups, and missing pets. But even more inviting than the colors are the images of people: brown men, women, and children, Ethiopians presumably, save a lone white man in sunglasses and a baseball cap playing a guitar. The top of the poster features two Ethiopians in flight: one grasps his shins in an acrobatic tumble, the other walks upside down in the sky.

The event is a fund-raiser for a nonprofit organization, Action for Youth and Community Change. This will not be a sober exchange of ideas, the poster promises. Instead it will be a celebration of "the Vermont/Ethiopia connection." Not only will there be, possibly, flying Africans, there will be Ethiopian food and music to accompany them. Most precious of all to me is the promise of an evening in an interracial setting with people happy to spend a night that way—people like me.

What fortune, I think, and write down the information. The scoreboard ticks: *Stay.*

"What brought you here?" I ask a young white woman I meet at my parents' church in North Nashville, where I spent every Sunday morning until I went to college, and whose congregation has always been composed mainly of students and faculty of Fisk University and Meharry Medical College, and therefore has been almost entirely black since its inception in 1955. The woman is new to the city, a recent transplant from Massachusetts.

"I am finding it difficult to lead an interracial life here," she says, meaning Nashville.

"So you came here for a dose of blackness," I joke. I

am immediately sorry when I see my words have embarrassed her.

"I understand," I explain. "So did I."

I was never able to live an integrated life in Nashville, either. My family lived two lives: a free life in the black world of North Nashville and a guarded one in the white world of South Nashville. It is one of the many pleasing ironies of my life in Vermont that here, in the second "whitest" state in the union (after Maine), for many years I lived in a neighborhood that was more integrated than the one in which I grew up.

"In the South, white people want you close but not high. In the North, you can get as high as you want but they don't want you close." I grew up hearing this maxim repeated by friends and colleagues of my parents throughout my childhood. The choice was easy for me. For as long as I can remember, I knew I would forsake close for high.

This formula has not been borne out in an absolute way in my experience, at least in terms of my life in the North. But the part about the South is uniformly true. While the South, like all of America, is still largely segregated, the lives of black and white southerners have always been intertwined, even though our relations have been more often treacherous than not.

On a late afternoon in the spring of 1985, I sat in a coffee shop adjacent to my high school. I was talking with Justin, a classmate, about our college plans. It was May and graduation was approaching. After working our summer jobs, we would both head off to schools far away from home.

Maybe the proprietor overheard us. Or maybe he was

drawn to the unusual sight of a white boy and a black girl sitting together in his shop, sharing doughnuts and laughing. For whatever reason, he came over to our table.

"How y'all doing?" he asked. He noted how much fun we appeared to be having. We told him that we would soon be leaving for college.

"California," Justin responded when the proprietor asked where he was going. He received an approving nod. I faltered when the man asked me the same question. I wasn't surprised when he said, "Now, why would you go all the way up there?" Justin laughed. I laughed, too, even though I felt a tremor of hostility underneath his question.

"Don't we treat you good down here?" He balanced his fists on his hips.

"Oh, yes! I love the South," I said, still laughing. "This will always be my home."

I went on about what I would miss, how cold the North was, how hard had been the decision to leave home. All the while I was conscious of his fists, and the way he leaned his torso toward me. His brows furrowed as he listened, but he wasn't really listening. Rather he was straining to hear a truth beneath my words, his eyes behind his glasses beaming like interrogation lamps. I kept my body rigid and waited for him to walk away. It was time to go.

But the man was right. I was hiding something from him: myself. "We wear the mask that grins and lies," wrote African American poet Paul Laurence Dunbar in 1890. Justin and I said good-bye in the parking lot. As I steered my parents' car toward home, I thought, *This is what I'm leaving behind.*

That summer I put thick black marks through the calendar days that separated me from the day when I would finally begin my life up north. But I could not leave the South behind. I still can't. James Baldwin said, "You never leave home. You take your home with you. You better. Otherwise, you're homeless." However uneasy is the history of relations between blacks and whites in the South, it has made me, and it claims me still, just as it claimed the proprietor of the coffee shop; we were ensnared in the same historical drama. I was forged—mind and body—in the unending conversation between southern blacks and whites. I don't hate the South. To despise it would be to despise myself.

The North was a dream that I borrowed from other people. In high school, I was allowed to take for credit a course on African American literature at Fisk University. I read slave narratives whose protagonists longed for northern states not only to escape slavery but for affirmation of their humanity. I was introduced to the African American literary culture of New England, as well as the Harlem Renaissance, many of whose greatest talents, like W. E. B. Du Bois, Nella Larsen, and James Weldon Johnson, studied or taught at Fisk at some point during their careers. I read the works of Du Bois and Johnson and their searing indictments of the hypocrisies of northern liberalism. I was undeterred. If I wouldn't be thoroughly content in the North, I figured, at least I would be freer than I felt in Nashville.

I visited my older brother in New York once during my high school years. He had an internship in the city for the summer and assured me that I was more than capable of finding my way to his office from the airport. I wrote out the route in painstaking detail: shuttle to subway to his office building. I was proud of myself when I found the correct subway stop. I lost my footing as soon as I entered the subway car.

It wasn't the number of people that disconcerted me. It was the sight of so many people standing close together—some touching, some standing face-to-face—and not talking. I felt as if I had stepped into a science fiction movie. In the South, at least when I was growing up, if someone passed you on a street and said nothing, it meant something.

Stranger still was the fact that even though they were not talking to or looking at each other, the subway riders were obviously aware of each other. On another subway ride that summer, I saw a woman step out of a subway car and then turn and shout that she had left her bag on the seat. One man held the door open while another man grabbed the bag and gave it to the first man, who handed it to the woman. *Thank you. No problem.* So they are human, after all, I thought, and felt tremendous relief. But that was it. After their acts of human kindness, the men on the subway retreated into science fiction silence.

Now I am one of the subway zombies. I've even mastered the tight choreography required to navigate a New York institution like Grand Central Station. The trick is not to look directly at the always-dizzying number of bodies zooming toward you. It can be disorienting, like looking too closely at the windshield when you're driving in the middle of a Vermont snowstorm. Today when I am in a subway car in New York, I grip the cold metal pole and look up and around and pretend I am alone in the world.

The slower pace of New England reminds me of the rhythm of the Deep South of my mother's childhood, a place with which I identify because it is, like New England, a place I know mainly through stories. I read *The Scarlet Letter* and the poetry of Emily Dickinson on family trips down to Mississippi, where I spent hours in the homes of relatives and eavesdropped as the women in my clan spun tales about the world.

John grew up in Lenox, Massachusetts. The neighboring town of Great Barrington was the childhood home of W. E. B. Du Bois and the site of the country home of James Weldon Johnson. I do not believe it is a coincidence that I fell in love with a man from the same geographical region as the settings in the books I read as a child. I recognized the topography of Lenox on the first day that John took me home to meet his family. We passed the hill where a young woman on a sleigh crashed into a lamppost and died a death that inspired Edith Wharton's *Ethan Frome*.

"I remember," I said. I had read the book in high school. The hill was much less impressive than the one in *Ethan Frome*. But I knew it. I knew the hill as it had imprinted itself in my brain and body, into the marrow of my imagination. It has always been impossible to separate the romance between me and John from the romance between me and the geography that produced him.

I felt at home in Lenox that day, and for over thirty years have called New England my home—where cemeteries sprout like fields of wildflowers and there is, always, a Main Street. I feel a singular affinity for the place, particularly whenever I am somewhere else and asked where I am from. My favorite high school English teacher complained that people use the word "love" too loosely. The same word, she said, could not possibly capture, for instance, one's feelings about one's mother and, say, ice cream. I use the word "home" just as promiscuously. I have used the word "home" to refer to hotel rooms, houses, apartments, and, on two occasions, a tent that wasn't even ours, but borrowed from my friend Estelle. There has always been a place to call home in every country, city, and town I have ever lived in or visited. But the places in which I have most felt at home for much of my life have always been somewhere else.

Unlike me, my daughters are at home in Vermont. "They are true Vermonters," I say of them so often that they have now begun to say it about themselves. I see it in their relationship to the natural world. By this I mean that they seem to believe that it is a good idea to wear shorts and T-shirts in sixty-degree weather. I sneak fleeces into their backpacks and enjoy the irony: my daughters were born near the Danakil Depression, yet here they are in South Burlington, undaunted by even the harshest winters. It took me many years of successive snowfalls to understand that I should come to expect snow in winter and not treat it as if it were a freak occurrence, as it is still treated in many parts of the South.

For my daughters, the experience of being black in a white place is not strange. To the contrary, it is an every-day fact of their lives. But there will most likely come a time when that everyday fact will mean more to them than it does now. For this reason, like other parents of brown children that we know, John and I take advantage of every opportunity to show our daughters that they are not alone.

Dark skin stands out in a white place. Hypervisibility has its drawbacks. Kiran, a young poet whose parents emigrated to Vermont from Pakistan, tells me that with wearing a hijab comes a burden of representation. "I always hold the door open," she says, "because I might be the only Muslim that person has ever seen." At the same time, the hijab makes it easy to identify and be identified by other Muslims with the same beliefs. To be visible is to be vulnerable to a particular kind of judgment, but it also makes it easy to identify one's kin.

In his 1953 essay "Stranger in the Village," James Baldwin recalls his experience of living in a small Swiss village whose residents had never before encountered a black person, a situation he had not anticipated. "It did not occur to me—possibly because I am an American—that there could be people anywhere who had never seen a Negro," he wrote. His first visit lasted two weeks; he assumed it would be his last. Yet he returned the following winter, and the winter after that. "But I remain as much a stranger today," he wrote during that second winter, "as I was the first day I arrived, and the children shout *Neger! Neger!* as I walk along the streets." His body fascinated the residents. His smile, hair, and the color of his skin astonished them. "In all of this," he continued, "in which it must be conceded there was the charm of genuine wonder and in which there was certainly no element of intentional unkindness, there was yet no suggestion that I was human: I was simply a living wonder."

In my first year of teaching at the University of Vermont, I had a young white female student in a class who had never spoken to a black person before she came to college. She saw a black man once at a bus station, she said, and wanted to start a conversation, but couldn't think of a good cover for her curiosity. At college, she quickly became part of a black community of friends. In fact, she was persuaded to tell me this story by two of her black girlfriends, who flanked her in class and teased her good-naturedly, clearly enjoying the story—so foreign to them—about what it meant to be white in a white place.

For many students, the experience of being a member of a minority group here is not easy. My friend Estelle works directly with minority students. She suggests that they view their college experience in Vermont as a four-year study abroad program. That particular option expired for me many years ago.

Estelle and her husband have lived in Vermont for over thirty years. When they arrived, there were only a few hundred black people in Vermont. They raised three children here, including two sons who have had damaging encounters with local police. A story of one of those encounters made the front page of the local paper. It has taken every day of those thirty years for Estelle and her husband to arrive at a point in life where they could call Vermont home.

African Americans who have lived in Vermont for decades have big stories to tell. Curtiss Reid Jr., a native of St. Louis, moved to Vermont in 1979. At the time, there were only four black men in the entire county. During the first six months of his life here, nearly every police officer he encountered would stop and interrogate him. It stopped when, eventually, he became known as "the black guy on the bicycle." When I ask him what the term "home" means to him, he says that home is a place where he is recognized.

Curtiss was six years old when he discovered the night sky. His mother had sent him to a camp in Eureka, Missouri. The view of the sky, unobstructed by city smog, changed him. He knew he would have a life in which the natural world would be at its center. He was once married to a black woman from Alabama who never felt at home here. When she accused him of loving Vermont more than he loved her, he did not deny it.

Curtiss shakes his head in amusement when I tell him about the scoreboard in my head. Like my daughters, he is a true Vermonter, and has dedicated his life to the place. He founded the African American Heritage Trail and serves as executive director at Vermont Partnership for Fairness and Diversity. His footing in the world of Vermont is sure; he has no doubt that this place is home.

I wish I were like Curtiss. I wish I felt his assurance, and that the glory of nature and the night sky were enough for me. I wonder often if my inability to feel at home here is a consequence of a general uneasiness that colors my experience of being in the world. I wish, too, that it didn't unnerve me every time someone questions my choice to live here.

"How do you do it?" asked a Brooklyn native recently after comparing the racial virtues of New York to the generally monochrome world of Vermont. She asked the question in the smug way of New Yorkers who believe that the cultural kaleidoscope of their world somehow confers upon them a special kind of moral rectitude. I felt a rush of bewildering emotions: distress, envy, and indignation. I

started to defend the place to which I have yet to feel alle-
giance. I wanted to show her a picture of the life I have built
here, a good one, with close friends, neighbors, students,
and colleagues, a job I enjoy, a house I love, and brown
children who are relatively safe. Such a picture would not
satisfy her, I knew: she would see only the whiteness of its
border. And no picture can capture the ineffable essence
of a life.

There were other pictures that I did not want her to
see. For instance, the image of me preparing to leave the
house I love, the care I take to make my body presentable,
the primping, combing, and the application of lotions and
pomades; the daily rituals I perform to conceal and reveal;
to curate the despised blackness of my body and cultivate a
respectable racial self that is always, like it or not, engaged
in the act of representation. Even a short trip to the grocery store is an event that demands this self-surveillance.
Yet it's never enough; no amount of grooming can protect
me, can assuage the continuous feeling of vulnerability.
The only thing that makes it bearable is the discovery that
others perform these rituals.

"You do that too!?" A friend and I lean back in our
chairs and laugh. Our laughter is honest and free. As we
confess our stories to each other, my heart fills with relief
to discover that the anxiety that had made me feel ashamed
and damaged is not unique. I am also aware of the irony:
without our mutual sense of alienation we would perhaps
not have this communion to enjoy.

How do I do it? Day by day, story by story, contradiction by contradiction, brick by fucking brick.

.   .   .

I couldn't do it without role models, black people who found a way to make a home out of this white place. Dr. H. Lawrence McCrorey moved with his family to Vermont in 1966 from Chicago, where he had been a professor at the University of Illinois. A job offer at the University of Vermont was promising, but so was the opportunity to keep his wife and children safe from the race riots spreading like fire through the city.

Larry was revered in our community. He was a doctor, professor, and an administrator of the highest rank. He was also an accomplished jazz musician, a saxophonist, and a poet, a writer of sonnets and limericks. When I met him, he was seventy-five and one of the most handsome and magnetic men I had ever met. He died in 2009.

John and I met Larry and his family at a dinner party at Larry's home in the spring of our first year in Vermont. We ate and drank heartily that night. After dinner, Larry treated us to a bawdy new limerick he had written. A few of us walked to the lake, which was about a hundred yards from Larry's house. It had been a tumultuous year for me. John and I had married that summer shortly before we moved to Vermont. My mother had been diagnosed with breast cancer. I had survived a bout of adhesions in my bowel that took a surgeon eight hours to untangle. I felt rattled in a global way, and I wasn't confident about any of the decisions I had made. But as John and I drove home that night, still warmed by the good cheer around Larry's table, I watched the night sparkle on the lake outside my window and thought, for the first time since I arrived, I can do this. I can make a life here.

I wanted my students to learn from Larry, so I asked him to visit my classes almost every year. He might have objected to what I was requesting of him, which was, on some level, simply to come and be a black man for my white students, some of whom had never been in a room with a black man, much less a man like Larry. But Larry did not object. He was used to it. When he arrived in Vermont, he was one of only two black faculty members at the College of Medicine, but his responsibilities extended well beyond the classroom. The university president depended upon him to mediate whenever a race-related problem arose on campus. He was asked to make speeches across the state about the racism in Vermont that lay beneath the state's facade of social justice. He was an activist by nature, but also by necessity.

For my students, he told many well-rehearsed stories. Stories about his life, including the racism he had experienced in Vermont. He described his work to end Kake Walk, a particularly odious fraternity tradition at the university, where white students dressed up in blackface and competed "fo' de cake." Larry told them that defeating racism was a continuous struggle but that we must always confront racism, which was ingrained in this country's fiber, and which had been learned but which could be unlearned, just as he had learned to untangle his own biases.

My students were awed by the handsome man with his thundering, sonorous voice and polished stories that did not coddle. One student, however, was visibly uncomfortable during Larry's stories about racism in Vermont.

"If it's so bad here, why don't you leave?" Her question was defensive, but I like to think she meant to ask its gentler cousin: "What makes you stay?"

"Because I love it here," Larry said evenly; he had

heard this question before. "This is my home." The student was silent.

I learned exactly what my students learned that day, which is that being at home does not necessarily mean being at peace.

Larry's visibility came with a cost. He received hate mail, some of which contained death threats. Over the years of dinners and visits to his home, he showed me one of the letters. I glanced at it quickly. The childish scribble itself was unnerving. His daughter Leslie told me that she found all of the letters neatly organized in a file in his office after her father died.

What does it take to make a home? I call Leslie and ask her not long after I ask the same question of my childhood friend Ellie. Home is family, she says. Vermont itself may not feel like home to her, but like many people I know, Leslie appreciates the fact that life here can be lived on a human scale. Incidents of racism that might be dismissed in cities with a higher percentage of African Americans are treated seriously here. When two young women of color in Burlington received flyers advertising the Ku Klux Klan, the incident inspired a downtown rally. Vermonters take pride in the accessibility of public officials. When I invite the Burlington police chief to visit my classrooms, he comes. He talks to my students about the importance of diversity on the police force. I am proud to show him off to my students, but sometimes I wish he were the kind of swaggering redneck I see on YouTube clips, an authentic, power-hungry brute for my students to enlighten and bring to heel. Our police chief may be an aberration compared to others in his profession, but his ethics are perfectly in line with the city he represents.

I like telling my New York friends about our police chief. I talk him up the same way others wax on about the mountains and the snow. But there are aspects of life here that I am inclined to leave out of my story of living black in Vermont, such as the fact that African Americans are consistently overrepresented in the state prison population. In fact, the Vermont incarceration rate of black men is the third highest in the country, proportionally speaking. And while no shootings have yet occurred, African Americans are 85 percent more likely to be stopped by the police than their white counterparts. Like the black body I work so hard to refine for public view, I find myself tempted to shape an image of Vermont that conforms to fantasies I have been nursing about New England since childhood. It is a temptation I find difficult to resist.

I can't stop thinking about Larry's hate mail. I think about the letters when I am at the grocery store or the post office or the farmer's market, wondering if the person ahead of me buying milk or stamps or handmade soap authored the hateful, menacing sentences about a man I loved and admired. I picture Larry reading them and calmly filing them away so that he would never be able to pretend that Vermont was not home to racists just as much as it was home to Bernie Sanders, whom he called a friend, just as he was a friend to the police officers and other public officials whom he alerted about the letters. Because the letters bore no return addresses, the police investigation went nowhere.

I want to do more than imagine what it felt like to read those letters. When I ask Leslie if I can see them, she puts them in a manila folder and gives them to me on a dingy spring afternoon.

It is midsummer by the time I read them. I choose to do so on a day when John and the girls are out of town. I park at the library, one of my favorite places in the city, and where I saw the poster for the Boogie Benefit. I walk down to Battery Park, another favorite place. I like this park because it is popular with the local community of New Americans. There are always children here from different countries and of different races. It is late afternoon. The setting sun fills me with dread. I sit on a bench and listen to faint strains of a clarinet playing "The Star-Spangled Banner" somewhere down the hill that leads to the lake. The plain, stiff folder sits beside me like an impassive stranger.

The language in each letter is chaotic, with ramblings about Jews, gays, and immigrants. One letter contains a newspaper clipping about Kake Walk with a photograph of Larry as well as a copy of a photograph of Adolf Hitler. "This a white state and the majority of the people want to keep it that way," reads one letter. "People like you will never be welcome outside of the South Bronx and Harlem."

The first worst thing about the letters is how recently they were composed, the latest in 2002. The second worst thing about the letters is how little their content surprises me.

I fold the letters up carefully and put them back in the folder. Everything is the same, I tell myself. It's the same Vermont as it was when I sat down on this bench. It's the same lake, which, in fact, belongs to me as much as it belonged to Larry, or anyone else.

A few years ago, I went to a discussion at the library about the concept of home. It was an installment of "Bridging Cultures," a series sponsored by the Vermont Refugee Resettlement Program, which was established to assist refugees and immigrants in becoming full participants in all aspects of American life.

What is home? I found the range of responses to the question intriguing. A young woman from Kenya described home as an imaginative space, a geographical container of memories. A man from Iraq reminded the group that for those citizens of the world who lack the safety of a physical structure, home is composed of the people with whom one shares one's life. For others, home was simply the place in which you were born. A man born in Nigeria described home as a sensory experience. A woman from the Caribbean described home as a place where one feels free to be oneself. "Home is the place where you feel safe," said a young woman from Somalia. Vermont was home to her, she said, just as much as it was home to a fourth-generation Vermonter who grew up on a farm in a rural town two hours from Burlington.

Once I reach the library parking lot, I tuck the letters under the debris of my daughters' old schoolwork and wadded-up snow pants in the backseat. Maybe we're safe here, or maybe we're not, I think. Maybe it's just a matter of time.

. . .

The view on the way to the Boogie Benefit is iconic. From our car windows, the Vermont of postcards and picture books stuns John, the girls, and me into silence. The beauty is relentless: grand, sturdy trees against dark, muscular mountains, and a boundless carpet of emerald-green grass. As we near Lincoln, a bright natural spring appears and accompanies us into the town. I always feel safe when John is at the wheel, but today I feel secured by this place—not the state or the town but the earth itself.

In Lincoln, Main Street takes us to Burnham Hall, where the Boogie Benefit is being held. Only as I stand at the threshold of the building do I consider the improbability of scores of brown bodies in this place. Only then does it occur to me that the advertisement, like most advertisements, probably will not live up to its promises.

So I am not surprised when I cross the threshold of the building and discover not a single Ethiopian in sight. I am not surprised, but I can barely suppress a giggle that rumbles up from my diaphragm and into my throat. John and I exchange sly glances over our daughters' heads.

I make a show of hustling my daughters into the room as a way to suppress the laughter. The hall is cavernous and comforting; its design is both pristine and primitive. The room is filled with people whom, after having lived here for seventeen years, I can describe with confidence as authentic Vermonters. They wear a state uniform: worn jeans, sandals or otherwise sensible shoes, and unassuming spectacles. Some of the men wear ponytails and faded patterned shirts. They are graying and middle-aged, gentle-looking and slender, with bright cheerful eyes. Young people chat in small groups throughout the building. One woman dressed like a flamenco dancer walks slowly through the center of the room.

Two brown children, a boy and a girl, enter the hall. They are as distinctly Ethiopian as the other guests are identifiably Vermonters. Like my daughters, the kids have round brown eyes, heavy, dark eyebrows, and cherubic lips. Their father wears a blue flowered shirt and a straw hat with a black band. He is white. I recognize him from the university. We give each other a shy wave. Giulia and his daughter approach each other and then disappear into another room.

Isabella is tired, too tired to eat, even though the four of us had been looking forward to the feast all day. A buffet table is surrounded by people holding paper plates sagging with savory stews and glistening sautéed vegetables. I try to convince Isabella to investigate the table with me, but instead she spreads her body across John's lap. She dismisses everything I bring her to eat but perks up when I present her with toasted seeds, an Ethiopian snack known as Kolo. "They taste normal," she says. John and I laugh. "I knew you would laugh," she murmurs, too sleepy to take offense, and begins a dreamy monologue about McDonald's.

The entertainment arrives. An Ethiopian singer wades through the audience, shaking hands with the men and women who gather around him. Isabella sits up to watch him and does not complain when I lead her by the hand to the stage.

"She was born in Ethiopia," I tell the singer when he leans down to greet us.

"I can tell," he says, and touches her cheek.

Before the music begins, the singer introduces himself and his band "for the newcomers." As I look around it becomes clear to me quickly that I am among the minority of people who have never seen him perform. The singer nods at the band behind him, and Ethiopian music quickly saturates the room. The stage is lit up with the energy of the performers. The space, which had seemed cavernous when I entered, is now tight with sound and bodies moving in concert. John bobs his legs, drums on his knees, and then gets up to dance. I ache to join him, but my desire is outweighed by my fear of becoming a spectacle: the only black woman on the dance floor. The days of watching myself sweat and shake to my favorite music in the mirror with my best friend are long gone. I haven't danced that freely in years, and certainly never in Vermont.

As I sit and feel sorry for myself, the woman in the flamenco costume finds a space in the center of the floor and reaches her hands up high, her eyes closed as she waves her arms slowly to a beat beneath the one that the rest of us can hear. She stretches one arm at a time, her hands spread and reaching up toward the light. She slips in and out of view as bodies bop and jerk around her. I watch her for a while and then close my eyes, too, and let the clap of music and the lingering smell of the food penetrate me and crowd out my memories and fears. Before the scene drowns out all thought, two sentences flash in my mind, their letters towering and spectacular: I am alive. I am safe. I close my eyes and give myself over to the small, full world that surrounds me, sure for once that in this night and this place, I have found, if not a home, at least a place to be.

Epilogue: My Turn

A few years after my mother died, I discovered a cache of papers she left in my childhood bedroom closet. She buried them, in an act of elegant and amusing symbolism, underneath a pile of my father's long-forgotten wrinkled shirts. The papers consisted mainly of poems, drafts and drafts of them, but there were a few essays. I hadn't known she wrote essays. One of them is an autobiographical narrative about her life as a child in the Jim Crow South. It's called "My Turn."

When my mother was a child she often accompanied her beloved grandmother, Mama Tempie, to a local grocery store. In order to get to the store, they had to walk past rental houses owned by a lumber company. One day, some white boys threw rocks at the two of them. A pleasant stroll turned into a "nightmare," my mother wrote.

Mama Tempie, who practiced the kind of black stoicism that has served as a guiding principle for African Americans since the inception of African presence in this country, walked on without evincing any emotion while the white boys jeered and pelted them with stones. When my mother asked Mama Tempie why they were being treated that way, her grandmother told her that the boys didn't know any better, and should be pitied instead of hated.

My mother idolized Mama Tempie. She accepted her grandmother's reasoning, and as an adult went on to practice the same kind of forbearance that made Mama Tempie the embodiment of strength and moral fortitude in the poetry my mother wrote. But the rocks still wounded; she wrestled with the wounds in "My Turn." Her grandmother's keen analysis of the nature of racism, that it was the consequence of ignorance, did not stem the flow of blood that ran down her leg.

After reading the story, I knelt on the floor, my heart racing. I reached the final lines and then started all over again. I was looking frantically for something. What was it? I didn't know, but I kept scanning the lines over and over, my throat tight and my breath short. There was something I needed that I didn't see. *What is it?* I kept asking myself as I read the paragraphs again and again, and then searched through her other papers, looking and looking. *For what?* Some words to correct the abomination of the rocks and my mother's bloody leg. And then I realized that what I was looking for was the salve, an answer, the end.

"For while the tale of how we suffer, and how we are delighted, and how we may triumph is never new, it must always be heard. There isn't any other tale to tell, it's the only light we've got in all this darkness," James Baldwin explains. It took me a while, it took the journey of this entire book, but I realized that there was a lesson, which was, in every scar there is a story. The salve is the telling itself.

"What did it mean for a Black woman to be an artist in our grandmothers' time?" asks Alice Walker. "It is a question with an answer cruel enough to stop the blood." But eventually the blood must resume its flow. We are helpless to stop it.

The hunger to tell is a drive I inherited from my maternal line. My mother's skill as a poet was something she inherited from her mother, who probably inherited it from another female ancestor, and back, and back, all the way to Africa. Unlike my mother and grandmother, I have been lucky to find interlocutors, hungry listeners, to borrow a phrase from *Their Eyes Were Watching God*, a book that looks like a novel about romance but is really a story about women, mothers and daughters, the primacy of intimacy and conversation, and a woman's fundamental hunger to tell. The body of the black woman at the center of the tale is the situation; the story is about how this black woman learns to become a storyteller. In order to narrate her own life, she needs another person to listen, to aid in the tending of her interior.

My mother never saw her work in print, but her stories course through me, just like what those stories represent, which is the vital importance of intimate connection across time and circumstance, which is why, I believe, she left her papers in my closet in the first place.

I found "My Turn" just as I was nearing the end of this book, and I kept it close as I composed these lines. It did not soothe me to have my mother's words beside me. Instead, it unsettled me. Even after I understood the subtle and complex lesson of her story, the need persisted in me for something easy: a happy ending.

Relatedly, I wanted, as I began to write these final

pages, to compose a particular kind of narrative, a neat trajectory from her turn to mine, the past to the present, despair to hope. But there is no simple path forward, and maybe the hope embedded in the stories I have told in this book is insubstantial and misguided, just as misguided as the racism that spurred white boys to hurl rocks at my maternal ancestors. But the need to believe thunders through my body and muscles out despair. "I can't afford despair," James Baldwin once said. "You can't tell the children there's no hope." But the beauty of the condition of blackness is that it is capacious enough to carry both despair and hope, rage and delight, ambivalence and fortitude, which are all as intertwined as my intestines and scar tissue, which seem driven to entangle themselves periodically, and form adhesions that serve as a regular reminder that the scar and the story are eternally connected. It is a process I am helpless to stop, just like the blood that courses through the interior of my black body.

Acknowledgments

I am pleased to have the opportunity to thank the people who helped usher this book into being. First and foremost, I owe a tremendous debt to everyone who allowed me to incorporate our shared experiences into these essays. In the instances in which I have received permission, I have used real names. In other cases, I have changed names and other identifying details in order to preserve privacy.

My heartiest appreciation goes to three people whose private lives intersect most deeply with my own. Thank you to my dear husband, John Gennari, and our daughters, Isabella and Giulia Gennari, for permission to share with readers stories from the lives we are living together. I am grateful to the three of you for putting up with my probing and musing. I apologize for the intrusion, but it's your own fault for being so interesting in the first place. Thank you, John, for your remarkable memory, stunning insights, and for reading, listening, and talking through everything. I know it isn't always comfortable to be written about. Trust me, I got the hint when you expressed much more enthusiasm for the pages in which you did not appear than for those in which you did. Still, you always encouraged me and never complained. I owe you, and I owe our daughters who, when once questioned about what it's like to be the subject of their mother's writing, sighed and said, "We're used to it."

I am privileged to be a member of big and loving families. I am grateful to my parents who are no longer alive but whose instruction guides me every day. My brothers, James and Warren, are my champions and friends. My aunt Julia shared family stories and supported my intention to take them to the page. Margarita Bernard and Joan Gennari Tyer have always been sources of unwavering support. Doreen Odom, your sororal support extends to your enthusiasm for my work; I appreciate your incisive feedback. A special thank-you to my cousin Renee Baron for your example and camaraderie along our similar journeys. I am extremely lucky to belong to a family in Ethiopia to whom I feel a gratitude I will spend a lifetime trying to come up with enough words to capture.

I am thankful for those people to whom I am connected beyond blood, family, and marriage. For early support, I am indebted to Faith Childs, Miranda Massie, Sandhya Shukla, and Heidi Tinsman. My confidante Davida Pines has always believed in every word. I am lucky to have enjoyed more than three decades of kinship with Ellie Des Prez. Thank you to my beloveds Hilary Neroni, Todd McGowan, and godsons Dashiell and Theo Neroni. Thank you to the Hurley family for always making space at your table for me and mine. Alexis Hurley, your generous and enthusiastic consideration of the essays in this book made it possible for me to clear many difficult hurdles along the journey.

Thank you to the many people over the years who listened to or read all or portions of this book and gave me crucial feedback. Greg Bottoms, you are a model as a writer and a teacher, and I am grateful for your consistent support over many years. I could not have had a finer writing partner than the precise and eloquent Lee Ann Cox. Thank you for opening my eyes to parts of the world I don't typically see. Anne Fadiman, I aspire to what you do on the page and behind a podium. Thank you for your critical insights and creative vivacity. Edi Giunta, your fine sense of what words can do inspires me. David Huddle, thank you for your patient nurturance, stellar example, and for believing in me always. I am fortunate to have the creative and intellectual support of Ethan Iverson. For many years, I have valued the keen mind and vision of Nancy Kuhl. Kathy Pfeiffer has always been a treasured friend and literary conspirator. Ken Schneider, I am grateful for your friendship and for the time and care you took with these stories. As a reader, writer, and human being, Lisa Schnell is scrupulous, dazzling, and fearless. Thank you, Bob Wilson, for making space in the pages of *The American Scholar* for my work, and for making me a better writer. Thank you, Louise DeSalvo, for the model of excellence you set in every aspect of your life.

When it comes to Elizabeth Alexander, I will have to let a few words count for many; otherwise, the particulars of my debt to her would take up an entire essay. I will say this: Elizabeth, thank you for your breathtaking example as a mother, speaker, and writer, and for opening doors, both real and imaginary. I falter, too, when it comes to adequate words of thanks for Major Jackson. I've got this: brother, thank you for telling me when I got it right and when I got it wrong. I owe a special debt to Kevin Quashie, whose gracious eleventh-hour literary heroics made me know that I was not alone. I asked so much of you, Kevin;

thank you for saying yes. Fortune shined on me the day we met. How lucky I am to know you, Alice Quinn, and to benefit from your immense generosity of mind and spirit. Thank you for believing, and for making it possible for me to believe. When it comes to championship, no editor surpasses Vicky Wilson. Thank you, Vicky. It has been my privilege to work with you. And thank you, Marc Jaffee, for tending so thoughtfully to all of the details. I am grateful to the very patient and skilled Nora Reichard, senior production editor at Knopf Doubleday. I thank my agent Gail Hochman for consistent support and enthusiasm.

My life in Vermont has brought me into close connection with so many fine human beings, many more than I can list here. But I must thank Beverly Colston and Patricia Corcoran for friendship and for reading. Leslie Wells, thank you for sharing your family and stories with me. Loree Zeif, I am forever in your debt.

I am grateful for my friends at Good Shepherd Lutheran Church, where I have enjoyed loving support and a platform to share my stories. For multiple opportunities to get to know a wider Vermont community of readers, I thank the Vermont Humanities Council. From the Vermont Arts Council, I received much more than institutional support, although I am particularly grateful for a Creation Grant that enabled me to focus on writing the essays in this book. I am thankful to the Vermont Studio Center and the MacDowell Colony for allowing me to benefit from the extraordinary worlds they create.

At the University of Vermont, I have been lucky to have had many fascinating and formidable students over the years, a few of whom conducted research for me while I was writing this book. In particular I thank Sophie Scharlin-Pettee and Megan Williams for helping me verify important details.

Throughout these pages, it has been my primary aim to stay faithful to the emotional authenticity of the experiences I explore in this book. In "Motherland," Helen Franklin represents an actual person, but ultimately the essay is about my own experience, and therefore attends to what I felt, heard, and saw over the course of our adoption process. While "Motherland" is an honest account drawn from information available at the time, Helen Franklin was never sanctioned for professional malfeasance, while individuals affiliated with the American agency were eventually prosecuted by federal authorities.

For permission to relate the story of how we became a family, as well many other stories in this book, I thank, again, my three: John Gennari and our children, Isabella and Giulia Gennari. Everything good in this book, and in my life, exists because of you. I am grateful.